D1589690

David Farrell was born in Glasgow in 1969 and became a professional footballer at the age of 16. His 28-year footballing odyssey took him to Oxford United, Hibernian, Partick Thistle, Airdrie, Clydebank, Stranraer, Albion Rovers, Gretna, Clyde, Dundee, Notts County and Celtic Nation as player, coach and assistant manager.

David's experiences have given him an insight into the realities of the game that few can match and his popular blog, 'Football From The Inside', has earned David a reputation as a witty, honest and incisive analyst of the game.

He lives in Glasgow with his family and drives a taxi for a living.

TAXI FOR FARRELL

FOOTBALL BETWEEN THE LINES

DAVID FARRELL

TAXI FOR FARRELL: FOOTBALL BETWEEN THE LINES
Copyright © 2015 David Farrell

Published by:

Teckle Books Ltd
Unit 15
Douglas Court
West Henderson's Wynd
Dundee
DD1 5BY

For more copies of this book, please email:
frank@tecklebooks.co.uk

Designed and set by Chris Collins

Printed in Great Britain by Bell and Bain Ltd, Glasgow

To my Mum and Dad,
for everything

The Early Years
1969-1986

St Mungo's Academy
Eastercraigs Boys Club
Chelsea Boys Club

I'm a recovering insomniac. Being buffeted and bruised by professional football for 28 years does that to you. The playing side, that's the easier part for most, although if you self-analysed as much as I did during my playing days, tossing and turning becomes a regular night time pursuit. However, coaching and management, that's a whole different ball game. You try your best not to take it home but it consumes you, night and day, week in week out. Twenty-eight years of it. I've experienced pain, adversity and, on the odd occasion, joy and I wouldn't have changed it for the world.

It would be a lie to say I wouldn't have loved to have played at the highest level of the game (and hoovered up the enormous trappings that went with it), but the truth is I got everything I ever wanted because I was able to say I was a professional footballer. Not only that, I survived for 18 years as a player before finally succumbing to the ravages of injury and a pair of legs that had 'gone'.

From a very young age my dream was to be a footballer but I never really believed I was good enough to 'make it'. The main reason for this was the high pedestal I put footballers on, particularly the Celtic players I worshipped from the first moment my Dad took me with him to watch them. Like a lot of young boys, I never thought about playing for anyone other than the team I supported. I knew I was the best player at my school but I also knew that was no guarantee of being good enough to make the grade in the professional ranks, let alone at Celtic. I didn't just want to be a footballer, I wanted to be a Celtic player.

I grew up in Dennistoun, just a couple of miles from Celtic Park. Although full of rogues and the odd sword-wielding maniac, it was as welcoming as the east end of Glasgow could be. I don't want to perpetuate the myth that it was a hard life or we had to fight for everything we had because that simply isn't true in my case. My parents would sometimes hold down two jobs each to make sure me, my brother and sister had as much as possible. Life was far tougher for them than it ever was for us. Throughout my career I cultivated an image of myself as a hard man on the pitch but, in reality, I've never been a fighter. There was trouble if you wanted it, but it was equally easy to avoid if you used your brain and I was always far too interested in playing two-touch, two-a-side or any other variation of the beautiful game to get involved.

By the age of 15 I'd sampled a gang fight once, mainly out of curiosity. The Dennistoun Monks (who I loosely belonged to through my more committed mates), gathered nightly at the bottom of the long and winding path which led to a bridge separating our territory from the neighbouring Royston Shamrock. On

10

this occasion, as I'm assuming with all the others, we chased them one way then they chased us back. To-ing and fro-ing from one end of the bridge to the other with hardly a blow landed in anger. And that was it. After 20 minutes I got bored and headed back to the school we hung around in for a game of football.

I never particularly liked school. It was a necessary evil and, although I was reasonably clever and did well enough to gain O-Grades and Highers, it was never a place I enjoyed going to. I also used my intelligence in a less academic way after realising fairly quickly that popularity wasn't handed to you on a silver salver. Fortunately for me, a lot of the school hard men also played in the football team and, being a good player, I was able to use that to my advantage as they'd need to rely on me on a Saturday morning when we went to the toughest of places to win. It was on those horrific red ash pitches that Glasgow is famous for that I learned how to use what I had to make my way in the game. Crashing into tackles, targeting their best player and then running over the top of him with bloody knees, and sliding into another challenge when you knew you were coming out with third-degree burns from ham-string to backside. It was the same recognition of what I was good at that was to carry me through my career. We had a good team that regularly won our regional league but there were times when I carried that team to victory. They knew they could trust me and, in turn, I got that trust back in spades if I ever got into scrapes in and around the school.

As the curtain began to close on my school years, the question of 'what comes next?' arose. Although there was only one real option in my mind, I dutifully filled in application forms for apprenticeships with various companies in the city. The school careers officer encouraged me to follow up on these applications, to my obvious ambivalence.

'Well, what do you want to be?' she asked.

'A footballer.'

'No,' she replied, trying to smother a condescending smirk. 'What do you REALLY want to do?'

'I REALLY want to be a footballer.' And with that I got up and walked out.

But I was still uneasy. The phone wasn't ringing. Clubs were hardly banging down the door for my signature and the self-doubt was creeping in again. By now I'd seen many of my contemporaries snapped up on schoolboy forms. My good friend Alex Rae, who would prove to be a pivotal figure in my career, was with Rangers. Others in the Glasgow schools' select squad like Paddy Connolly, Gary McSwegan, John Spencer, Alex Cleland, Stephen Frail and Sean Sweeney had all gone to senior clubs. Stuart Balmer, David Elliot and Gerry Creaney would all go on to represent Celtic. And that was just the Glasgow area. All over the country there were players with lofty ambitions and, in many cases, more technical ability competing with me for an ever-diminishing number of opportunities. Football doesn't open its books to many each year and most of those lucky enough to find themselves in the vice-like grip of a coveted 'S' Form will never get near a professional youth squad. Most again will fall by the wayside over the next couple of years and only a fraction will go on to carve out any kind of career in the game.

12

At just 15 I knew I was falling behind and I could see my dreams slip away. But I was still determined to do the very thing that everyone had told me wasn't possible. I HAD to be a footballer.

Ask a stranger about Glasgow and chances are they'll talk about football. Or sectarianism. Or both. For better or worse the two are inextricably linked and in Dennistoun you were one or the other; Protestant or Catholic, Rangers or Celtic.

My school was St Mungo's Academy and our own Old Firm derby was against our great Protestant rivals, Whitehill, whose star player happened to be Alex Rae. I relished the passion and hatred of our games and clearly remember one clash at their place that had been arranged for right after the school bell. This ploy meant their pupils would pour out and line the side of the narrow, red blaes pitch for the 4.30pm kick off. To some it would have been a terrifying, intimidating prospect. I couldn't wait. Alex would be in direct opposition and, while he was their talisman and leader, his supporting cast was nowhere near as good as he deserved. In my heart of hearts I knew I wasn't as good a footballer as he was, he was technically better than me, so challenges like this were vital for me to prove I could at least mix with the best. Despite Alex's best efforts (he managed to score a double for a poor team) we destroyed them. I scored two and laid on three in a 7-2 victory that saw me snarl and scream my way around the pitch, charging into everything and anything above the ground. We expected the Whitehill mob to be waiting for us when we came out, to stone our minibus and teach us a lesson for coming to their place and running amok. It never happened. Our margin of victory had been so great that, by the time the seventh had gone in, there was barely a five-a-side team left at the school gates, never mind a baying mob.

That day showed me I could handle intimidation and threats of violence coming from the sideline, something that would stand me in good stead when I faced both sides of the Old Firm as a Hibs player. In my first game at Celtic Park I came on as a substitute fairly late in the game. Having mainly played reserve football to that point, the majority of fans would have been unaware of my background. Peter Grant had possession next to the old 'Jungle' and I came across and timed a great tackle, playing ball and man and knocking it off Granty for a throw-in. Both of us ran for the ball, trying to 'buy' the throw-in from the ref. I grabbed it and tried to take a quick throw, only to hear a voice in the crowd denounce me as a 'fucking Orange bastard'. I looked up at Peter, who was still trying to grab the ball from me, and we both smirked wryly at the fan in question.

Two seasons later I was playing at Ibrox and, by now, was slightly better known. We had a corner early in the game and I caught a header flush from six yards that flew just past the post. I should have scored. Scoring in front of the Rangers fans at the Copland Road end was something I'd fantasised about but, as my momentum carried me onto the track, my dream became a nightmare. Only yards from my face a blue sea flashed a variety of one- and two-fingered salutes accompanied by the usual 'wahaaaayyyyy' and

14

'you're shite ya Fenian bastard'. Celtic and Rangers fans tend not to do shades of grey so in that context my house was a hotbed of diversity.

My Dad was from Royston, or 'The Garngad' as it was known in those days, which was a very staunchly Celtic (i.e. Catholic) area. However, my Mum was a Protestant and her family were very active in the Orange Order, with my aunts and uncles regularly taking part in walks and processions. They do say opposites attract, although it has to be said my mother never once had any involvement or interest in that side of things.

Growing up, sectarianism was very prevalent and yet it was never as much of an issue as it is in today's politically correct world. Certainly not in our house nor those of my many Protestant friends. Despite the rivalry there was never any apartheid in the streets of Dennistoun. We hung around together, joked around together and played football together. And, with my desperation to be a footballer, I played more than anyone else.

At the same time as I was fretting about my prospects in the game I was actually earning the admiration of one of Scotland's top clubs. Unfortunately for me, that club turned out to be Rangers and, with my background falling foul of the club's signing policy at the time, I was quickly ruled out in their eyes. Although I didn't know it at the time, this bigoted approach to recruitment was to help change the course of my life.

Certain youth coaches, it's fair to say, have an over-inflated sense of themselves. You can see it any Sunday morning as middle-aged men with initials on

15

their manager's jacket, and coaching certificates they wield to prove they're the next Guardiola, scream and bawl at kids who just want to play football. It can be seen at professional sides as well. For too many, wearing the tracksuit and being able to tell people they're the coach of a big club, is more important to them than producing players. My experiences after signing for 'Chelsea' certainly backed this up.

At that time there was a strong Scottish identity at Stamford Bridge, with people like Kevin McAllister, John McNaught, John Millar and David Speedie around the place. This was something they wanted to build on and were keen to set up a satellite centre in the west of Scotland. Their Head of Youth Development, Gwyn Williams, approached me to captain the newly formed Chelsea Boys Club, who would recruit all the best unsigned players in Glasgow, with those who proved themselves good enough going on to sign for the London giants.

I'd been with the well-respected Eastercraigs Boys Club since the age of 12 but, three years later, it was time to move on. With professional teams now sweeping up all their best players, Eastercraigs were finding it difficult to compete and I needed a team who were going to be successful if I was going to catch someone's eye.

We all signed up and got our Chelsea bags and ties, t-shirts and a ball. I was even invited down to Stamford Bridge for a trial. In truth it was nothing of the sort, more of an Easter Holidays visit. Big clubs are good at that. Making you feel they're giving you an opportunity, whilst fulfilling their obligation to take some of the boys down for the Easter Week. At the

16

end of that week, I asked the manager of our team, David Skinner, if there was any possibility of it going further. 'Of course, you've done well,' he said. I had, but I also knew he was fawning me. Skinner was a salesman not a football coach. He was an Arthur Daley-type and, even then, I knew more about the game than he ever would, but he did his job in one sense. He sold us all on the club, the bright lights and the glamour. I've got a feeling he got more out of being associated with Chelsea than we ever did. The nagging, onerous self doubt started to creep back in as I realised that no professional form would be forthcoming. Surely it wasn't to pass me by. I couldn't let it go. I HAD to be a footballer.

Chelsea swept all before us on the park, winning our league convincingly and reaching the Scottish Cup Final against Celtic Boys Club. This was the big one, as I knew there would be plenty of scouts at the game. At 16 the football scrapheap beckoned, but there was no way I would allow my last chance to pass without a fight, to meekly accept amateur football and an apprenticeship with Weir Pumps.

We lost 2-1, but I had a stormer, scoring our goal, running red ash-scarred legs all over the bumpy grass (grass: a luxury!) and straining every sinew in the hope that someone might recognise my potential. The next day, our house phone rang more often than a stockbroker's in a Wall Street hotel room. Clydebank and Motherwell offered two-year apprenticeships, Hibernian and Dundee United trials. In 24 hours I'd gone from afterthought to sought-after but there was still a curveball to be thrown from a city better known for scholarships than apprenticeships.

The weekend following the cup final saw us play in an international tournament in Ayr as I mulled over the various offers on the table. After the first game, I was walking back to the tented administration area when an elderly and very dapper-looking gentleman tapped me on the shoulder.

'David?'

'Yes,' I politely replied.

'My name is David Coates. I'm the chief scout of Oxford United Football Club.'

'Oxford...United?' I mumbled.

This was a team who had just won the Milk (League) Cup at Wembley and who were playing in the top division in England. This could be a game changer. My heart pounded. I tried to play it cool, but I'm sure the excitement in my voice would have given me away.

'We'd like you to come down for a week and have a look around.'

This was to be no 'Stamford Bridge' look around, this wasn't even a trial in the strictest sense of the word. I could tell by the way he was talking that they liked me. I was going down there so they could convince me to sign. I never gave the consequences a thought. Leaving home, leaving Dennistoun, leaving my family and all my pals – none of it came into my head. All I could think about was getting down there and proving myself.

As it turned out, Dave Coates had bumped into an old scouting friend at the tournament. Alistair Stevenson, who was head youth scout for Rangers,

18

had been aware of me for some time and had seen us lose the Scottish Cup Final to Celtic. He thought I was a decent player but I couldn't be recommended to his employers so he mentioned my name to Dave instead. A tap on the shoulder and I was to realise my dream after all. And, incredibly, had Alistair Stevenson not shown sensible discretion, I could even have been a Rangers player.

Nah, maybe not!

Serving My Time
1986-1988

Oxford United
Scotland Under-18s

Every player wants to play at the highest possible level. It's something fans don't understand when their star striker up and leaves for a bigger club. Suddenly, the object of their adulation becomes all the bastards under the sun. Only doing it for the money and lacking ambition, they reason. Content to sit on the bench and watch their bank balance grow.

The thing is, opportunities to move up the ladder don't come around very often in football, as I was to discover later in my career. Almost without exception, players are always looking for their next move. If a bigger club comes in for them then they have to believe in their ability to cut it at that level, even if the chances of warming the bench are higher.

This was my reasoning as I ruled out Clydebank after suddenly finding myself hot(ish) property. They were a well-run club, but Motherwell were higher up the footballing food chain. It was to be a straight fight between the top division in Scotland and the top division in England. I headed down to Oxford for a week to play two pre-season friendlies. It's important to stress at this point that I was going down there as a youth player, someone who they could potentially bring through to their reserves and hopefully, at the end of it all, 'make it'. I was still a long way from being a footballer.

I quickly had to settle in and made a conscious effort in that first week to be as friendly as possible and keep my mouth shut. This was probably the most difficult thing for me as I'd a tendency to air my opinion, something that was to cause me a major problem later on at Partick Thistle. But, for now, I was the model apprentice. That first week was to turn into three as I played match after match to a good standard and quickly showed I could hack it with their existing youth signings. I also made sure I became an affable lodger as I was to be housed with a family for the duration of my contract. The Jaycocks – Jackie, her husband Barry, and their son Aran – were to be my new family. Homesickness was for cry babies. If ever I was feeling that way, I would never let anyone see it. I couldn't face the embarrassment of having to tell people I was nearly a footballer once but I'd given it up because I missed my Mum.

And so the contract was signed. I informed Motherwell of my decision and I signed with Oxford United for the princely sum of £40 per week, rising to £45 in the second year. My wages were only two or three times what I could have made on my paper runs back home, but I couldn't care less. I was training to be a professional footballer, doing something I loved. I made a quick visit home to say my goodbyes and collect my limited belongings but, rather than this being a wrench, I couldn't wait to get back to Oxford and play football. This was the real deal and I was ready for it.

When you became an apprentice back then, you were assigned a duty. As well as doing the boots of four first-team players, everyone had their area to clean. The boot room, dressing rooms, corridors, and tunnel areas were each the responsibility of a group of trainees. It's a far cry from today, where clubs employ boot men and cleaners and kit men to do all those laborious tasks and protect their mollycoddled trainees from missing a development match due to a broken fingernail. As well as looking after 12 pairs of boots daily, my task, along with two others, was to look after the away dressing room – cleaning the showers, walls and hoovering the carpets after training and matches. We'd be there until five or six o'clock every night making sure our own particular patch was spick and span.

Match days were incredible back then as Oxford were playing Man United, Liverpool, Spurs and Arsenal on a regular basis. We would wait outside the dressing room after the game for the nod from Kenny Dalglish, Alex Ferguson or George Graham to go in with brush, shovel and black bag in hand. I'd be sweeping and picking up the discarded bandages and rubbish around the feet of suited and booted stars like Hansen, Rush, Molby, Robson, McGrath, Rix or Adams as they waited for their team bus to come up the narrow alleyway at the side of the Manor Ground. On the odd occasion the stragglers would come waltzing out of the showers and, as you bent over to retrieve the last of the strappings, you'd have Norman Whiteside's hairy arse flashing uncomfortably close to your head. You can imagine the weekly phone call home that night with my parents eager to catch up on anything unusual and a rundown of the day's events. My Dad used to keep a diary of my time at Oxford, but I'm not sure there was ever an entry describing my dressing room chores, thankfully. I'd be trying not to catch those superstars in the eye whilst clearing up but, at the same time, I'd make sure I said something, anything, to my fellow trainee within earshot of any of the Scotsmen sitting there. And I made sure the accent was cranked right up.

'Where ye fae wee man?' was the usual response to my excited ramblings.

'Dennistoun,' I would reply, always forgetting the 'Glasgow' bit first.

'Shuts on a Friday night and opens back up on a Monday. Bit rough there, wee man, eh?'

I couldn't open my mouth to fire back a quip, but that was okay because I was too starstruck to think of one. I would still be pretending I was in on their joke as they went back to discussing the day's events and the evening's activities as I swept and hoovered around their gleaming shoes, careful not to touch the buffed leather. They were still the 'Untouchables' in my eyes. Cucumber-cool, or at least as cool as I could manage while almost pissing myself with a mixture of anxiety and delight, I continued on my merry, midgie-raking way. Inside I was screaming 'KENNY DALGLISH!' while taking it all in.

Our apprenticeship duties kept us close enough to the big time to know it was there for the taking while reminding of how far we still had to go. My experiences of mixing (albeit not quite as equals) with King Kenny and co. just made me want it more. Should the bigger clubs ever go back to this way of working, it would go a long way to deflating the egos of young, talented prima donnas who think they've made it before the ink dries on their first contract.

Oxford had their own star names as well. Ray Houghton, John Aldridge, Dean Saunders and Tommy Caton had been signed for hundreds of thousands of pounds, and training with them in that very first week made me recognise my weaknesses and how far I was from the first-team squad. I felt the self-doubt creeping in again, but thankfully this time it was to be used as a strength. My attitude and desire, will to win and strength of character had to be second to none if I was to have any chance. Most of all I needed to look after myself off the pitch and make a lot of sacrifices, because if I was to slip one inch, I'd be found out. In my mind the fight had only just begun and I had to find some way to outpunch my opposition.

Footballers are all thick. Their brains are in their feet. They were at the back of the queue playing keepie-ups when intelligence was being handed out. Everyone knows it. The only problem is that it isn't true.

The stereotype of the stupid footballer annoys me because I'm not stupid. That's not to say I'm any kind of genius either and when I began blogging about my experiences in the game I was nervous about what people would make of the uncensored scribblings of someone with no formal writing experience. The overwhelmingly positive reaction surprised and delighted me, although there was one back-handed compliment that stuck in the craw.

Graham Spiers, a journalist I have huge respect for, said something along the lines of, 'I thought he was just a deranged madman who had escaped from Carstairs on the pitch, however this is a very good read'. The perception seems to be that because you'll scrap and fight your corner on the pitch, that'll you'll kick your granny off the end of a four-man wall to be the one to take a blockbusting free kick square in the chops, that you must be thick.

Spiers is a magnificent writer and clearly a very clever man, but why can't he see past the stereotype? Why give with one swish of the pen and take away with the other? I'd love to sit down and talk tactics with him. Then we'd see where the football intelligence lies.

This deranged madman had to show huge levels of football intelligence, and indeed life skills, throughout his career. He had to identify not only his own strengths and weaknesses, but also those of others who were a threat to his chances of making it. I wanted to be a footballer so badly that I would, and did, systematically take down my main rival for a higher place in the Oxford United pecking order. I was strong and aggressive, but I also had a very good positional knowledge of the pitch. I could 'see' things before they happened and put myself in the right place defensively. It was part of the reason I was a good defender. You can't always teach that type of intelligence. I've worked and played with many players who you could put through technical drill after drill and they still couldn't take it in. But put them in front of goal or up against it in their own box and they instinctively know where to be. That wasn't me. I, like most of the people in the game, was a thinker and when I arrived at Oxford I quickly assessed the other trainees in my position. Only one had a chance of getting a contract ahead of me at centre-half so I made him my target. Luckily, I'd identified a chink in his armour that I would use to elevate myself up the ladder. I would have to make myself the brawn and the brain.

Darren Britnell was a local lad. Rangey, relatively strong and well liked among the pros. To someone from the east end of Glasgow he was a bit of a silver spoon type, who displayed supposed aggression with a Tim Henman-like fist pump. I could see through it and knew that, for all his physical attributes, Darren was what my future Hibs manager Alex Miller would dismissively call 'perfect son-in-law material'. He was now my target. If I could push past him into the reserves, I'd have a better chance of getting a contract. So I did everything I could to prove I was the better bet, manipulating things to ensure I was always on the opposite side. I would pick him up at set pieces in full-scale practice matches and beat him in the air, or at least be physical enough that he didn't get a free header, and if there was ever a 50/50 challenge there was no way I would come out of it the loser. In possession games, where there are no goals and the only way to beat your opponent is to retain the ball for a certain amount of passes, I'd try to make sure I was closest to him when he received it so that I could get a tackle in or he'd give it away as he was under so much pressure. I would never have deliberately hurt a teammate but I made sure I could expose his weaknesses at every turn, all to prove to the manager and coaches that I was a better centre-back than he was.

And then, it happened.

At clubs up and down the country there is a weekly ritual whereby players sit and wait after training to hear the squad announced for the Saturday match. The assistant manager will come out with the sheet in his hand, protecting it as if it was the Bayeux Tapestry, and sally toward the noticeboard in slow motion to prolong the ceremony. The players, for their part, will try to catch the eye of the coach, looking for any indication of a change or something different, but nothing is ever given away. A dozen or so players will know they're in the squad, mainstays who saunter up to the notice only to check meeting times or the name of the hotel they'll be staying at. Four of five will go up, anxiously checking to see if their name is on the list, hoping they might keep their place. Outcasts and those coming back from injury already know their fate but, still, they check.

This time, it was a Thursday afternoon and the first-team were leaving for Old Trafford the next day. A nice overnight stay in the Post House Haydock meant a 2pm Friday departure. As apprentices, we had to get all the kit, boots and equipment ready before we finished work on Thursday night. The usual formalities ensued as the first-team coach Ray Graydon entered the changing room. Only there were fewer players in the scrum than usual as the club was in the midst of an injury crisis. I'd only played half a dozen reserve games and never even gave the list a thought. Darren, however, did and scanned down the names.

11. *Houghton*

12. *Brock*

14. *Phillips*
(clubs rarely use 13 as a kit or squad number)

15. ***FARRELL!!!!!***

I swear, he must have scanned it four times to check they hadn't made a mistake and put in the wrong name ending in -ELL. He walked away shaking his head muttering 'I might as well just ask to be released now'.

'Aye, you might as well,' I replied, with a straight, serious face, but he thought I was being sarcastic and we joked about it for a minute before I left him to wallow in his anger. I couldn't have any sympathy for him, could I? It was part of my plan, although I didn't expect it to bear fruit so soon. Back then there were only two subs, so I knew I'd be spare man on the bench but it didn't matter, nothing mattered. I was going to Old Trafford. At 17. And I'd be sitting there, in the dugout, AS A PLAYER.

We finished around five o'clock that evening and, as I made my way home with Derek 'Stan' Tully, an Irish lad who lodged next door to me, it suddenly dawned on me that I'd need a suit for the journey to Old Trafford. In Dennistoun, suits were for weddings and funerals and, in my heightened, cloud-nine state, I'd forgotten that I didn't have one. Stan was from a similar background and notorious for his scruffiness, but a family wedding earlier that year meant his formal wardrobe was more extensive than mine. His dark grey suit clashed spectacularly with my light grey shoes (the only pair I owned) and the fact he was smaller than me meant it was a tight fit. The trousers stopped well above my ankles and showed off my pristine white socks. I can only imagine what my Dad and Uncle Charlie were thinking as I presented myself to them at the team hotel looking like something out of Kajagoogoo. It was a huge sacrifice for my Dad to be there as it was the day of an Old Firm game and he didn't miss them for the world, but it seemed that me sitting on the bench at Old Trafford would do as an ample, if a little more sedate, substitute.

That day was to be the closest I ever got to playing at the very highest level but to have even got that far, and to stretch out a career into almost three decades took, I think, a bit of brain power. That doesn't mean I stood out amongst my fellow pros though. I don't think there are any more or less stupid, or clever, footballers than in any normal working environment. But mastery of calculus or knowledge of Shakespeare isn't the important thing when it comes to football. You need the football intelligence or that natural ability to be in the right place at the right time, or do things with the ball others can't. I couldn't manipulate the ball well enough to compete with the top players and I was clever enough to realise that. I just had to use what I had to my advantage by stopping strikers and midfield players having a greater influence than I could.

Darren was a likeable and unwitting foe, but he wasn't an undeserving one in my eyes. I knew this thing could be over in a matter of months, or it could turn into something approaching a career and no one was going to stand in my way if I could help it.

We don't live in a world where people leave school at 15, go down the pit the next day and stay there until retirement anymore. People change careers with increasing frequency so, even if I never work in football again, the 28 years I got out of the game could hardly be seen as a short career by modern standards.

While your playing days are always a finite proposition, there are more opportunities than ever before to prolong your career in the game – in the media, as an agent, coach or even a (spit) referee. There are also more ex-players looking for ways to stay involved than ever before. To succeed in this increasingly competitive market you need to be committed, determined and focused. From early on I wanted to be a manager. The stress and the power of the position, the leadership, the shaping of a team and being the man who made all the decisions appealed to me. It's something increasingly unlikely to ever happen but, if I was ever to fill the big chair and make decisions about who to buy and who to sell, the character of a player would be as important as their ability. I want to know they'll stop at nothing to win. I want to know how they'll react to losing.

The football side of things was going well in that first year at Oxford. I'd established myself in the youth team, had my Old Trafford experience, and was playing the odd reserve game at places like Stamford Bridge, Highbury and White Hart Lane.

It was with the 2nd XI that I made my way to Brighton's Goldstone Ground, a tremendous, rundown remnant of the halcyon days of pre-Sky football with an old-fashioned stand and terracing on three sides. The first-team had a midweek game against Manchester United, so the youths were sent

33

to the south coast that Monday night like, as it turned out, lambs to the slaughter.

Reserve games were a chance to go toe-to-toe with established names coming back from injury or suspension and, sure enough, I passed a familiar, well-worn face in the tunnel. Big Doug Rougvie was an intimidating, colossus of a man, but he was also Scottish and, as we've already established, it was my policy to ingratiate myself to token Jocks wherever I found them in England's green and pleasant land.

'Awright big man?' I asked, with an implausible mix of confidence and fear.

'The fuck you wantin'?' was about as much as he could muster through that familiar gap in his teeth.

I spluttered a 'nothing' and made my way out. As I looked around the pitch, it quickly became clear that Rougvie wasn't the only big name out there. Digweed, Chivers, Dublin, Curbishley, Armstrong, Bremner, Penney. We were to be playing Brighton's first-team, temporarily demoted by manager Alan Mullery to punish them for a poor result and performance at the weekend. A hammering was inevitable and the 8-0 final score was to be the worst result in my career in professional football.

The sombre bus journey back to Oxford was made worse by the fact I was under instruction to report back to my Dad when I reached my digs. It was the pre-mobile and internet era and the next day's Daily Record was unlikely to carry reports from the Division 1 Combination League. The 1am phone call was an awkward one. The fact we weren't exactly expected to win when pitting our inexperienced wits against Brighton's first-team cut little ice with my old man. He was of the belief that no professional football team should ever lose by such a scoreline and he let me know it.

My Dad was a strong, strict disciplinarian who feared no one. He made sure we knew right from wrong, laying down all the principles of hard work and fairness I still stand by now and he managed to do it without ever laying a finger on any of us. The respect, and sometimes fear, I had for him is summed up by the time I was ordered off for Hibs at Links Park, Montrose for a stupid tackle when we were winning a Scottish Cup tie comfortably. I stayed out and never went home until seven o'clock the following evening because I dreaded walking in the door to face him. I was 24. A far cry from the supposed hard man you may remember from my playing days.

Partly through my Dad's influence and partly through my own innate desire to win, I hated losing. Many footballers find looking in the mirror and being self-critical the most difficult thing of all, preferring to blame their teammates, the crowd, the pitch, the formation, the physio or the hairdryer for not being hot enough. Some players will jump off the team coach and immediately forget they had just played a game. That wasn't me. I'd nothing but disdain for players who would break a smile rather than respect the joyless silence that accompanied a heavy loss, the same for a minority of others who secretly laughed and joked their way through the defeat. I felt it the night of the Brighton hiding and I felt it throughout the 27 years that followed. There's a right way to win, making sure you do so with humility and respect, but equally there's a right way to lose. Whatever people thought of my abilities I would never allow them to think I gave anything less than my all whenever I stepped on to the park, whether it was in the reserves or a cup final. Unfortunately, circumstances were about to prove what I already knew – that will-to-win wasn't always enough.

Training, for the most part, doesn't change. From my trial at Oxford in 1986 to my last stint at Celtic Nation in 2014, very little has been done differently. The world over, week to week, content is the same. Everyone does passing drills, everyone does possession games, crossing and finishing, shooting drills and small-sided games. There are slight variations but, in general, sessions follow the same pattern. Where it becomes different is in the coaching and the execution. How you set your team up and the positional play, as well as how you combat the opposition. Top-level players and clubs will all do very similar drills to those at the lower end, the difference will be that the top players can do them to a higher standard, more quickly and with more quality and intensity, and then transfer and execute while being put under pressure in a game situation. The point about how players of differing standards cope is vital, as I was about to discover.

I continued to make progress throughout the year that followed my Old Trafford 'debut'. Even though I would only catch the briefest glimpse of the first-team again – an appearance in the squad for a Zenith Data Systems Cup match – I continued to do well and had established myself as a reserve player. I'd even forced myself into the Scotland national Under-18 set up, although injury was to hold me back, something that would prove to be a feature of my career. I was forced to pull out of squads against Holland and Germany before finally taking my place against Wales in a Euro Championship Qualifier.

This was a big achievement because you rarely got in a squad unless you were signed by one of the big clubs. Nepotism has always been rife in our international set-up. At 16 I had trials for Scotland and never got near a squad yet there were players from Celtic and Rangers, who I knew I'd outplayed, that were practically guaranteed a place. This time I wasn't giving up my chance and played with a severely poisoned toe. I borrowed a boot which was a size bigger to ease the discomfort slightly, but still had to come off after 75 minutes. When I removed the borrowed boot at the end of the game, it became apparent I shouldn't have played at all as my toe had swollen so badly it resembled a blind joiner's thumb. I missed the next month's fixtures at Oxford as the poison was drained from my toe and was in excruciating pain, but no one can ever take away that cap and 75 minutes in a Scotland jersey. I felt that another call-off would have seen me branded injury-prone and unlikely to get another chance. I wasn't one of the fashionable names in the squad so I could quite easily be discarded. I couldn't let that happen.

Oxford had started to struggle in my second season there. Aldridge, Houghton and others had been sold and the manager started to come under pressure. The problem of smaller clubs cashing in on their better players and being unable to replace them with the same quality is age-old and ongoing. It's a balancing act and managers are having less and less of a say as chairmen up and down the country dictate signing policies. League position has to be taken into consideration when faced with an offer for your best players. If you put your club in danger of relegation by 'cashing in' on all your assets, surely it's just a false economy.

Like many before him and many since, the Oxford chairman Robert Maxwell, whose fraudulent business practices were to earn him posthumous infamy, had no clue about football. He saw selling three players as a way of bringing about a quick buck, not terminal decline. The manager Maurice Evans was hung out to dry as the inevitability of relegation crept up with as much stealth as a spirit at a Derek Acorah séance. I'd been given subtle indications under Evans that I would be alright. You know as a player when your time at a club is up. There are always signs – a higher squad number, losing your place, other younger players getting a chance before you – but I hadn't got any of them. I was sure I was in line for a contract until the day he was sacked and then it all changed.

A new manager was brought in to save the day and stave off relegation, someone who was to become as famous off the park as he'd been on it. Unfortunately, it was for his TV punditry and not his tactical knowledge that he was to make his mark after hanging up his boots. Mark Lawrenson was a Liverpool legend. I'd hoovered up his moustache clippings in the away team's changing room, but that was about as close as we were to become as he immediately declared the first-team wasn't just his priority but sole concern. This was understandable given the team's position, but a bad sign for myself and the other trainees approaching the end of our contracts.

From the outset, Lawro was intent on establishing a Liverpool at Oxford. He proudly proclaimed, 'we are going to train and play the Liverpool way'. It turned out that Liverpool was an exception because their training did deviate from the norm. They never had the structure most sessions do because they didn't need to do the drills we did. The side contained some of the best players in the world, those blessed with scarcely believable ability. They didn't need to work on shape to stop better players from hurting them like we did. Liverpool's players instinctively moved about the park, we needed to work on where to be and when. All Liverpool players needed was to play practice games to keep them ticking over, ours needed constant work on set-pieces, shooting and defending – the basics that might add a few per cent at either end of the park, turn defeats into draws, draws into wins and relegation into survival.

But the manager couldn't grasp this. We trained each day for 90 minutes, the Liverpool way. We had 5-a-sides in training, the Liverpool way. We changed the shape of the team so we could play the Liverpool way. We played... the Oxford United way. Someone had forgotten to tell him we never had Hansen at the back, Souness in the middle or Dalglish and Rush up front. Very often, great players like Mark Lawrenson don't make great managers because the game came so easy to them. With their natural ability they don't need to think about how the game is played, they just do it. Us mere mortals have to think about every single aspect of the game; from positioning, to how we can win more headers, to what goes on behind the scenes at clubs – everything that can give us just that little advantage to get us to the next level.

I was given my 'sign' in the run up to the last game of the season. The team were already down so Lawrenson had decided to blood a youngster and went with Eddie Denton. Eddie was a great pal of mine so I was genuinely pleased for him, but the decision to thrust him into the first-team squad stunk of a manager in trouble, desperately trying to appease the fans by giving a local youngster a chance. I still had the formality of being called in to the managers' office to come, but I knew my time was up. Even now, I can't remember hearing exactly what was said, but I know it wasn't 'when would you like to sign your new contract?' I got up and walked out, no discussion and no time for condescendence. There was a reserve match to play at Craven Cottage the next day. To this day, that game is a blur. The only clear memory I have is going to the bathroom at half-time to make sure my team-mates never saw me welling up as I reflected on my new-found status. I was 'free'.

Sunshine on Leith
1988-1996

Hibernian

At 18 I'd been discarded like a sweaty sock on the dressing room floor. I comforted myself in the knowledge that many better players than me had been freed from their first club and still gone on to have decent careers in the game. That was all I was asking. I didn't want to be Maradona or even my new pal Dalglish but I still desperately wanted to be a footballer more than anything. 'Pal' has a very ambiguous definition in the east end of Glasgow so, while we had never swapped numbers at the end of our five-second chat, it was clear to me we were now firm friends

I was trustworthy, energetic and a winner and I was determined those traits could get me somewhere. Playing reserve games at White Hart Lane, Highbury and Stamford Bridge against people I'd only seen on Match of The Day – Adams, Metgod, Rosenior, Dixon, Mabbutt, Dorigo and Hazard – made me hungrier than ever. I knew I could never be as good as them, but I also knew I could be someone. It was still down to me.

My initial huge disappointment quickly gave way

43

to determination. If I thought I wanted it before that was nothing to how I felt after getting tantalisingly close to the big time. Football is the most narcotic mix of joy and pain. All those feelings you have as a supporter – the agony, the desolation, the anger, the sheer unadulterated relief that comes with an important win, the happiness and the camaraderie that follows - I've had them all. Except, as a player, the hits are shorter and more intense. It doesn't last as long because, as a supporter, you have it in your heart. It's ingrained, it's YOUR club and you take it with you everywhere you go, for days on end. But the highs, for a player, are ecstatic, and the last-minute defeats and after-match lows, can be crushing. There has long been a perception among fans that players don't care and, while there can be the odd occasion where it may seem to be the case, it's rarely true. Playing football may not be time-consuming when you tot up the actual hours of a working week, but it is ALL-consuming. The training and looking after yourself, the scrutiny and the continual self-analysis, they all take over your life. It's a job and, when you're not at the top end of the game earning the big bucks, you have to make ends meet like everyone else. Oh, and you still have to remember to pass the ball to someone in the same colour of strip as you when you get it.

As soon as I was back up the road I took matters into my own hands and wrote to every team in the Premier League at the time, with one notable, light blue-wearing exception, explaining that I was a free transfer, where I'd been playing, my background, and asking for a trial during pre-season. In truth, I probably didn't need to get the Bic out, as any manager or development coach worth his salt would have been aware of who was available that summer, but I felt it would look good if people could see I'd taken the time to write to them and shown the desire to get back in the game. Football is a very small goldfish bowl and, while everyone knows everyone else's business, managers will go to great lengths to keep up the pretence that they have a better knowledge than the rest. After a short break I was back training and pounding the streets of the east end. Five-mile runs three times a week just to keep myself in good shape, something I would continue to do throughout my career. I was never blessed with natural fitness and had to work very hard to maintain a level that allowed me to compete.

Fortunately my begging letters paid off and offers of pre-season training with Motherwell and Dundee United and a trial game with Hibs were forthcoming. United manager Jim McLean phoned me personally and subjected me to an interrogation that wouldn't have been out of place in Guantanamo. He examined every part of my game. How was my right foot? My left foot? Was I good in the air? Quick? Could I tackle? No worries there. Would I move up to Dundee? Was I fit? All manner of questions about my overall game. I answered as honestly and as frankly as I could, although I had to strike a balance between being truthful and putting him off altogether.

I was offered a one-year professional contract on the back of my showing at pre-season training at Motherwell. I'd been honest with them from the start and made them aware of the other clubs' interest and Tommy McLean, Jim's brother and the Motherwell manager, was happy to let me go to see the others. After all, it wasn't Ronaldinho they were trying to sign.

I headed off to Tannadice the following Monday along with five other trialists from the West Coast. While I was there my parents told me that Hibs had agreed to match the Motherwell offer of a one-year professional contract and would wait until I returned home at the weekend for my answer. The knowledge I was at least going to still be a footballer no matter whether I impressed or not allowed me to relax and perform very well over the course of the trial.

The other trialists and I were summoned by Mr McLean to his office on Friday afternoon. One by one the trialists entered, like guilty criminals awaiting their sentence and one by one they came back out, only stopping to shake their bowed head. All of them were sent packing like dog shit flicked from a shoe as I waited to go in last.

Clearly I'd outperformed the others as Jim McLean wanted me to come back for another week's trial, which I wasn't adverse to until he added, 'but only if you tell those other two clubs that you're no longer interested in signing for them'.

I was taken aback. He was only looking after his own club, his way. He may even have been testing my commitment, but he was effectively bullying me and I told him politely that I couldn't possibly knock back two contract offers on the strength of another week's trial. With that, he got up, shook my hand and walked me to the door. I'd said no to Jim McLean, one of the greatest ever managers in Scottish football and he wasn't going to let me dwell on it. I'd now overstayed my welcome and with that, I walked out.

I had the other McLean brother to face a few days later. I went in and told him I'd made my decision, that I was going to sign for Hibs. I felt I'd a better chance of progressing there as they had a great reputation for bringing through young players. Motherwell's squad was ageing and they seemed to rely on experienced players more. On top of that Hibs were a bigger club and that swayed me more than anything else. Although he was gracious, I could see Tommy McLean was angry when I muttered my decision to him. I could easily have telephoned his office to do the dirty deed but they had been very good to me in allowing me to train and play some matches so it was also important to me that I travelled in by bus and train to tell him my decision face to face. My Dad wouldn't have allowed me to do it any other way.

The country is littered with failed footballers who didn't have either the intelligence or tenacity to realise their potential. I've lost count of the number of people I met in bars over the years who proudly proclaimed that they were a better player than me. My usual riposte was that they were probably right, followed by a polite 'what are you doing with yourself these days?' Very few ever got the irony.

And now I was going to be a Hibernian player, playing at Easter Road and Celtic Park and Ibrox, Tynecastle and Pittodrie. I'd stood on the terraces of them all, the biggest grounds and the smallest ones and now I was going INSIDE them, to the changing rooms, the Players' Lounge, the Directors' Box, the dugouts, the boot room and the big, communal baths that you only ever saw pictures of when someone had won the League. Getting into the bath with a fellow, hairy-arsed centre-back was the least of my worries. The journey to being a professional footballer was starting all over again.

I was to go on to spend seven and a half years at Easter Road, but in truth I was only really a first-team player for four of them. For the first three and a half I was a reserve, trudging all over the country on a Saturday and very often on a Monday night as well. Windy nights in Arbroath where the seagulls got more touches of the ball than I did, and wet nights at Forfar where young wannabes would try and kick lumps out of me after a day in the tractor, were all the same to me. I was a full-time professional footballer, as long as I could still say that I was like a pig in the proverbial.

I was back living with my folks and travelling through to Edinburgh every day with other Glasgow-based players like Graham Mitchell, George McCluskey, Joe McBride, Tam MacIntyre, Alan Sneddon and Pat McGinlay – guys I'd watched, even supported. We'd arrive at the training ground and more often than not go our separate ways, me to train with the 'stiffs' and the rest to train with the first-team. Being a full-time pro also meant I now had someone doing MY boots and getting MY training kit. Living the dream right enough.

In my 18-year career I would only make around 300 first-team appearances. The figure is disappointing but understandable given the relative few I notched up between joining Oxford at 16 and becoming anything near a regular at Hibs. The fact my leg muscles resembled Cheestrings and would tear just as easily by the age of 28 didn't help either. The frequent, painful comebacks from injury saw me back with the stiffs time and time again, meaning I probably notched up another 300 2nd and 3rd XI appearances. I'm not just well qualified to talk about reserve football, I may be the world authority on the subject.

While we did our stint at Gayfield, Recreation Park and Bayview, we also ran out at Ibrox, Celtic Park, Tannadice and Pittodrie, experiencing the dressing rooms, hospitality and big, demanding pitches. I played in Ian Durrant's comeback match at Ibrox, a reserve match in front of 15,000 people. There were Reserve League East cup finals, derby matches where the fringe players would be going hammer and tongs in front of a few thousand fans. Just like at Oxford, it showed us what was waiting for us if we had it within us to make the grade.

For me, there were few negatives to playing in the reserves, but that didn't mean I was happy to stick around there forever. More than anything, reserve team football makes you hungry to see the back of it and force your way past those you're playing alongside.

It was during my extended stint with the reserves that I was drafted in to the first-team squad for the first time, for a game against Aberdeen. I wasn't worried or even that nervous as I didn't expect to play. It was the 25th of August 1990 and Alex Miller pulled me aside, just as we were about to go into the team meeting.

49

'You're starting tomorrow.'

The instructions I received in the meeting took me by surprise. Centre midfield, man-marking Jim Bett. Alex had recognised that, at 5ft 10in, I was going to struggle to be a centre-back. I was excellent in the air, but sometimes even having a spring like Zebedee couldn't compensate for the difference in height to giant strikers like Mark Hateley or Aberdeen's Willem van der Ark. I'd played midfield in the reserves a few times, but it wasn't my position. I couldn't manipulate the ball well enough in there, or see the passes others could, but Alex knew I would have a right good go, and I did, but with no real thought or direction. We got battered 2-0 and, had it not been for Andy Goram, it would have been six or seven. I remember getting a touch of the ball in the first minute and another one in the 70th minute just before I was taken off. I charged about aimlessly to little or no effect and there may well have been some touches in between, but it certainly didn't feel like it. Meanwhile Bett strode effortlessly across the pitch spraying passes and dictating play in a manner I could only have dreamt of. I couldn't lay a glove on him. It was a harsh lesson and, with it, all the self-doubt that I never really belonged in that company came flooding back.

I remained in the team for the midweek trip to Kirkcaldy to face Raith Rovers in the League Cup, more due to the fact we were still struggling for numbers than anything else. We had Rangers at Ibrox the following Saturday and, if I wanted to be involved in that, I'd have to show more than I did at Aberdeen. It was a better performance than Pittodrie for me personally, although one or two senior players let us down and we were on the wrong end of a cup shock.

Another harsh lesson was to follow as I learned that the young player is ALWAYS the fall guy. It's an episode that has played out on many occasions over the years when a team full of senior players has underperformed, and yet the one who loses his place is the young player. I hadn't been great, but on that occasion I at least knew within myself that I wasn't the worst on the pitch but with players coming back for Ibrox, not surprisingly, I was under pressure. It always amazed me how some players would struggle to be fit for an away game at Stirling Albion on the Wednesday but would make miracle recoveries to be fully fit for the glamour game at Celtic Park or Ibrox on the Saturday. I certainly wish I'd been privy to some of those unprecedented cures through my later injury-ravaged years. That was in the future though and in August 1990 I was headed back to the stiffs.

Clearly I wasn't ready but, if I was going to play in the Premier League, it was going to have to be as a midfield player. I knew I was a good enough defender, but I wasn't tall enough to be as dominant as I wanted to be. I could fill in there now and again, but that wouldn't be enough. The problem was I didn't think I was a good enough midfielder to play there at that level. I didn't have the composure to make telling passes or retain possession under pressure. I couldn't manoeuvre the ball quickly enough out from my feet to a position where I could pick the best pass in tight situations. Somehow I'd have to do it differently. I could only be a ball-winner, aggressive and intimidating, stopping the playmaker and generally being the type of player people hated playing against. That way I could make a contribution and as long as I kept it simple, I could get away with it.

The reinvention of David Farrell – mild-mannered, quiet and as close to a pacifist as you get in Dennistoun – into a 90-minute snarling hard man continued apace.

Being a footballer isn't just about ability. Even the biggest hammer throwers need to be able to pass the ball from A to B after smashing into the opposition's best player sometimes but mental and physical toughness is often the difference between failing to reach your potential and playing above the level your talent merits.

I'd always loved a tackle and used my aggression to my advantage, but now it wasn't to be just a big part of my game. It was to be my whole game if I was to make an impression in midfield.

Gordon Rae was a bit of a Hibs legend and was coming to the end of his time at the club, but the knowledge he passed on to me when I played alongside him for the reserves was invaluable. Big Gordon taught me that you can't win every tackle and that you don't always HAVE to tackle.

'Faz, you know those flash strikers that like to play keepy-up with the ball and try their fancy flicks that make you look stupid?' he asked me rhetorically.

'Well I play keepy-uppy wi' strikers!'

He may well have, but by now a whisper in the

centre forward's ear warning that if he took an extra touch the next time the ball came up to them they'd be his next keepy-uppy victim, was often enough.

The fact intimidation could be used as a weapon was something I carried through my career as I used anything I could to get an edge on my opponent. Most of all I loved the feeling of crunching bone against bone, boot against shin pad and that masochistic, overwhelming pain when you both went toe-to-toe for a ball and the crowd squirmed and half turned away, squinting back just in time to see if there were any casualties. I often ended in a crumpled heap, only to jump up pretending I wasn't hurt, ready to go again.

Myths have grown up around the notions of sportsmanship, discipline and the bending of the rules in football. Shirt-tugging, sneaky fouls in 'good' areas of the park, off-the-ball stuff – we all tend to apply different standards depending on what side of the decision our team is on. Managers love to say 'I'm not one for wanting players sent off', but I've played for a few who would have allowed you to do almost anything to get opposition players wound up, whilst publicly trotting out that old line. They claim they'd take action if any of their players dived like their opponent had yet they never do and will also at least tacitly approve if it wins them a penalty or draws a red card.

Not long after signing for Hibs I started to pick up on the tricks of the trade, the sneaky, ugly, dishonest side of the game from the older pros. I could intimidate and manipulate situations with the best of them, but I wasn't a cheat, although my principles would be tested to the limit in the professional game.

My Dad and I sat in the living room one night watching the highlights of a Celtic game on Sports-cene. Paul McStay took a pass and strode elegantly past the first defender and, as the next one came across to challenge, managed to nick it from his dangling, outstretched leg. It was as clear a penalty as you'd ever see, or at least it would have been had Paul gone over the centre-half's leg and made sure there was contact. But McStay, being the man he was, skipped over it and, in doing so, lost his balance just long enough for the ball to run harmlessly into the goalkeeper's arms.

'What's he doing?' I said.

Dad sat up, startled and a bit miffed because you didn't interrupt my Dad in the middle of the football, least of all a Celtic game.

'He should have gone over his leg, made sure he got clattered and got the penalty.' I clarified.

'What?'

His tone and manner led me to believe he wasn't happy but I ventured further, hoping he hadn't understood the technicalities of my assertion. I explained further...

'He should have bought the penalty, the defender left his leg there and gave him the chance...'

My explanation was brought to an abrupt end. 'Don't ever let me hear you saying anything like that again...BOUGHT the penalty??!!'

I was severely chastised, in fact he slaughtered me. He was immensely proud of the fact I was a professional footballer, but would only continue to be if I

54

did things the right way. It was a lesson learned in morality and integrity, attributes that are all too often lost in the clamour to succeed, particularly in football.

I'm not sure I would be able to play these days as a lot of my challenges would be deemed reckless and careless, but they were more controlled than they appeared to be. They were well thought out and executed in order to play the ball and, at the same time, let my opponent know I was there and, furthermore, the next time they flashed their fancy-coloured boots in my direction I'd be there again. As much as I loved the physical side of the game and enjoyed opponents fearing me, I never wanted to hurt anyone. If they were between me and victory then there was a chance of becoming collateral damage, but I can honestly say I only ever went over the ball once in my career — the sending-off at Montrose that left me terrified to face my father and that still haunts me to this day.

My moment of madness came with 20 minutes to go. I controlled a pass, overran it, and their tall, rangy midfielder came hurtling toward me. At that moment, the player in possession is in danger of being hurt as he's lost control and needs to stretch to regain the ball, so I slowed up and waited for his tackle. It never came. He pulled out and my foot rolled over the ball and caught him on the shin. I was trying to protect myself as I really thought he was going to injure me but, in all honesty, I'd 'topped' him. I never even had the guts to look at the referee. I just got up and walked straight off. I was as driven as anyone to be a professional footballer, but I wouldn't sacrifice my principles to get there and my own interpretation of hard-but-fair was starting to pay dividends anyway.

55

It would be 18 months after my debut before I really had the chance to establish myself again, although one or two fleeting first-team squad appearances scattered between many reserve ones and a tremendous League Cup win for the club (which I wasn't part of) continued to whet my appetite. New Year's Day 1992 and a derby against Hearts was to mark a fresh start for me. My second baptism of fire saw me play at centre-back rather than midfield but the manager knew this was one occasion where I wouldn't let him down. The Edinburgh derby, in all its guts and glory, was to become a feature of my progression over the next four years; the type of game that suited my 'style'. Alex Miller knew he could rely on me to get stuck in and fight my corner on a freezing cold, wet night at Tynecastle. The game was significant in that it was the first Edinburgh Derby shown live on satellite TV, but viewers looking for entertainment would have better switching to Sky One as the ball probably had more bruises than the players by the end of the match. Honours were even in a 1-1 draw, but it was important for me as it marked the time when I finally felt as though I was ready. I contributed hugely in a match where Hearts had played a particularly physical strikeforce up front. I relished the battle and at last I felt I could hold my own in that company, even at centre-half on occasion. After four years of sweat and toil and a couple of hundred reserve games I was finally a first-team player, not just in name. For the first time I actually believed it. And belief is absolutely essential in football.

✳

56

A sports psychologist friend of mine once told me the key to winning big football matches was 'fire in the belly, ice in the mind'. You need the desire that makes you work that fraction harder than your opponent, but you also need to play with your head and not let the occasion overwhelm you.

In my time at Easter Road, Hibs finished third in the league once and were in the top five another five times. We won the League Cup (I didn't play) and were beaten finalists (I did play) a few years later as well as reaching a couple of Scottish Cup semi-finals. With excellent players like Andy Goram, Jim Leighton, Mickey Weir, Pat McGinlay, Keith Wright, Murdo MacLeod, Kevin McAllister, Michael O'Neill, Steve Archibald, Darren Jackson, and Brian Hamilton at the club we were certainly no mugs.

My job in that team was to stop the opposition's better players from performing, then get the ball to our own better players with the minimum of fuss, an arrangement that suited me. I wasn't to try anything fancy and I was delighted to be effective enough as a midfield spoiler to allow me to play in a very good Hibs side that regularly gave Rangers and Celtic very tough games.

But nine times out of 10 class will show and giving them a tough game isn't enough. Other than the League Cup final, when we beat Dunfermline, any time Hibs reached the last four of a cup competition one of the Old Firm was lying in wait.

It's a simple equation. If your team has better players than the underdog, then you should win. Big shocks happen less often than you might think and only get the attention they do because of the rarity factor. If their preparation and attitude is correct the favourites should never really be in trouble.

Attitude encompasses a lot of factors – desire, commitment, will-to-win, character and complacency. If any of those factors drop below a level where they overcome the ability to perform to something near their best, the big team are in trouble. My limitations meant I had to snarl and plough my way through reserve players just as readily as I did Paul Gascoigne to survive, but other, more technically gifted, players can occasionally find it difficult to mentally 'get up' for a game against weaker opposition.

It's difficult for fans to understand this as we expect our players to be up for every game, but it's unfortunately a natural human facet (even weakness) that is difficult to overcome. On the other side, human frailty means that teams going to Ibrox and Celtic Park often have an inferiority complex, no matter how hard they try to overcome it. Being able to play for the big clubs is about being brave with the ball, carrying it forward and making passes while dealing with the pressures of the crowd, the club and the occasion as well.

So coming up short against massive clubs like Rangers and Celtic was no disgrace, but there was no doubt that our derby record was a black spot on my time at Hibs. Over a five-year period, from 1989 to 1994, Hearts went a record 22 games unbeaten against Hibs and I'm still embarrassed to say my record was five defeats and three draws.

There was no question in my mind that in many of the derbies I took part in we had better players. There would be games where we dominated for 90 minutes and yet we still couldn't win, the most devastating example being a Scottish Cup tie at Easter Road. We were all over them but couldn't score and, as the minutes wore on, there was a horrible sense of déjà vu and the home support grew edgier. From an attack where we could've won it, a breakaway up the other end saw the inevitable Hearts winner with 87 minutes on the clock. They'd done it again, turned us over and I'd never felt so bad after a defeat. On reflection, we deserved it and we deserved a lot of the results in that period because we never changed our approach to the derby and the difference between the two teams was mental. We treated it like just another game, Hearts went to war.

We felt we had better players and believed our football would win in the end. We should have gone toe-to-toe with them, man against man, warrior against warrior, because there were times when that was all that Hearts team did against us. They had very good players in their own right, but when it came to the Edinburgh derby, there was a certain way to win it and they knew how.

As a team, I never felt we were ever as fired up as Hearts were. They were snarling and scratching in the tunnel and on the pitch they were pressing all over us, with players like Sandison, Black, Kidd, Mackay, Levein and Robertson galvanising and pushing each other. Make no mistake, they were angrier than us. They were ready for a derby, ready for a scrap. That's how they did it and the longer we went without beating them the more difficult it became, mentally as well as physically.

Fire in the belly, ice in the mind.

✳

My trial match for Hibs had been a friendly at Arbroath. We won comfortably and I slotted in fairly easily at right-back. While it wasn't my natural position I didn't see this as detrimental to my chances of getting a deal, but rather an opportunity to show that I could not only play, but also do so in different areas of the park. Versatility is an attribute generally looked upon favourably by clubs because having a player who can cover a few positions will inevitably save them money and allow them to concentrate budgets on the matchwinners, one of which I certainly was not.

I was a good pro who was never going to cause major trouble; I could be trusted and relied upon if needed but, most of all, I was relatively cheap. A player like that is great to have around. As I was to find out when I became assistant manager at Dundee, an extra addition to the squad for a relatively low wage is invaluable. Jump to the top of the game and the perceived wisdom is that big clubs need to have two top players for each position but it's not always the case. John O'Shea won't go down as a Manchester United legend, but he won five Premier league titles while playing more than 250 games for them. If O'Shea had ONLY been a very good centre-half, full-back or midfielder then he wouldn't have achieved nearly as much as he did, but the fact he could fill in in all these positions and on both sides of the park meant Fergie certainly knew his worth.

O'Shea won't have been one of the bigger earners at Old Trafford, but will have earned more in half a

60

week than I ever did in a whole year at the peak of my career. For all the reputation that footballers have for greed I bet money was always the furthest thing from John O'Shea's mind whenever he stood in the tunnel ready to do battle.

At that level, players aren't motivated by money when they go on the park because their contract guarantees them an obscene amount of money whatever the result. Very few people would turn down those type of figures if someone is willing to pay them it, but what keeps driving players at the likes of Manchester United and Chelsea is the prospect of winning Champions Leagues and League titles, of being the best in the game. What drives people below that is the opportunity to prove themselves at that standard and maybe even get themselves into that elite company, and so it goes on down the ranks as everyone wants to play at the highest level they can.

Some players playing at the level I was at were unquestionably motivated by money above all else, but they were in the minority and it's more understandable when the rewards on offer aren't particularly substantial. That wasn't me though. I was motivated by the fact I wanted to play football. I loved playing football. I loved the whole scene and if I wasn't playing I would be watching. Most players are like that, I think. They're motivated by their inner desire to play and win football matches. There is a third category of those not particularly bothered about being a footballer, who don't particularly hurt at defeat or experience joy in victory, but we're really talking a tiny percentage here.

From that first Edinburgh derby I played in through

to the end of the 1995/96 season I was at least an established member of the first-team squad. Whilst I was holding my own and playing with a bit more maturity, I knew I was still easily dispensable, as proven by the fact I'd usually be the go-to guy when we had a poor run of results and there was to be a scapegoat. My wage had rocketed up to £300-£350 per week, so it was easy to see the attraction for the manager of keeping me at his disposal. I would rarely rock the boat too much for not playing. Had I been forceful in trying to get more money it would have been easy for the club to say no and punt me out the door. I was useful in that I could be trusted to perform in more than one position, but it wasn't as if there was a shortage of other journeymen out there who would jump at the chance to play for a club like Hibs.

It was a fine balancing act and one I was to continue to do every time it was time for contract talks. I was well worth what I was earning now. I knew I wasn't as well paid as most in the team but, relative to a lot of people I knew, I was still earning a good living and win bonuses of £300 made me feel like I had Brewster's Millions. I'd played 200 reserve games to get here and was happy with my lot. I didn't need the 16-bedroom mansion or the Bentley. I'd reached my utopia of being a professional footballer in the Scottish Premier League. My two-bedroom flat in Dennistoun and a Vauxhall Astra were just fine thank you very much and, as our top earner at the time was probably only getting between £800-£1000, it's not as if I was missing out on sackfuls of cash.

On the park I continued to charge around and use those intimidation tactics when I could but I still struggled with possession in tight areas. I would know what the right thing to do was but, under pressure from opponents, I found it difficult to compose myself enough to take a touch or try and beat someone. I developed a style of play that allowed me to survive as I'd already have a look to see who was available and play the pass first time, sometimes into space and sometimes to a player. It worked because, as long as I was doing the other parts of the game – pressing, hounding, tackling and generally being a leader – I wouldn't need to be on the ball as much.

Good players have a habit of making you look silly at times, and not just opponents. Even your teammates can have a disdain for you at times because you can't handle the ball as well as they can. Because of that, they'll occasionally give you the ball in tight situations, knowing that you'll find it difficult to deal with. Michael O'Neill was a brilliant player with two great feet and a fantastic mastery of the ball, but I started to suss out that he'd occasionally do that to me. We used to joke about it in the dressing room afterwards.

'Why did you give me it there when I was under so much pressure?'

He wouldn't answer but would just look up at me as if to say 'you know why'.

In hearing this you might think the two of us never got on but Michael was a good pal during my time at Hibs. Footballers are very selfish creatures and what he was doing was looking after himself and, by extension, the team by making me prove I was up to it and wouldn't let him and the others down. Michael dropping me in it helped me greatly because it meant I had to start seeing the picture on the pitch quicker,

63

which usually meant me sticking the ball in the corner for the strikers to run on to and get it as far away from myself as possible. My wrath would then be directed at the lazy strikers who hadn't read my lump into the corner. I'd look across at Michael and he'd be shaking his head, knowing fine well what I was up to. I'd started to look after myself. I was learning the hard way and starting to carve out a niche for myself. I'd finally arrived and wanted it to last forever. I wanted to play in every game so, for that reason, I've never got my head round one of the most bizarre incidents of my career, my only experience of a player threatening to refuse to play in a match. And to make matters just a little worse, it was a goalkeeper.

For some reason over the years I've developed an aversion to goalkeepers and have even been accused of being something of a 'Goalie Hater'. It's nothing personal – I just hated losing soft goals and, because of that, I can be ultra-critical of those at fault, including myself.

People sometimes talk about keepers as if they're a breed apart because of the specialism of their position but the truth is that they're still only one-eleventh of a team and no more or less important than anyone else in the side.

Despite what the goalies' union – who always close ranks on those from outside who dare question their members – say, I believe I'm well qualified for the position of critic having played with three of the highest profile goalkeepers ever to have graced the

Scottish Premier League. Andy Goram, Jim Leighton and John Burridge were all very different types of goalkeeper and three very different types of character.

Andy attracted attention although he rarely sought it. Big Jim despised attention and tried everything possible to avoid it. John 'Budgie' Burridge craved attention and did everything he could to attract it! His idiosyncrasies and training routines were to become the stuff of legend and, while I got on very well with him, a lot of his antics did my head in. Budgie will always be well remembered by Hibs fans, particularly for being part of the League Cup-winning team, but being honest he was some way off Goram and Leighton in the goalkeeping stakes.

Budgie had all sorts of incredible wacky rituals, like insisting on arriving at training on a moped. We're not talking a Lambretta here, but the type of bike that a pizza delivery boy would have knocked back as unfit for purpose, but it allowed Budgie to drive through town being noticed and waving at his adoring fans. He was a tremendous enthusiast and extremely madcap, but I always felt a lot of the playing up to fans and swinging on the bar was an act to hide his deficiencies. He'd tell us how, in order to keep his mind sharp and his reactions at a premium, his wife used to sit with oranges and apples on her lap and intermittently throw them into the middle of the living room without warning for him to dive from his chair and catch. Tables and chairs were deployed in bizarre training routines where he'd kick the ball off the furniture from short range then attempt to make a reflex save because he never trusted players not to mishit a side foot volley and therefore mess up his goalie practice. I pointed out that strikers couldn't take tables on to the pitch and asked what he'd do if a striker mishit a volley but I don't remember ever getting an answer.

The likes of Budgie are easier to admire from the terraces and there was no doubting his entertainment value but it was clear Alex Miller hated his persona and Budgie didn't particularly like the manager either. Their fractious relationship came to a head on a visit to Airdrie's old Broomfield ground. Budgie had an old, worn and tatty jumper that he used to wear instead of a goalie top. It was made of heavy cotton and looked like something a farmer would plough fields in, but Budgie wore it for every game, swearing the ball stuck to it better than the sleek synthetic shirts we were sporting. We had new sponsors at the time and Alex was keen for the goalie to wear the shiny, bright new jersey with their logo on but, of course, Budgie was having none of it. The argument had been simmering for a few weeks and boiled over when we arrived at Broomfield and it was discovered the Farmer Brown shirt had been replaced on the dressing room peg.

Budgie was furious. He was screaming that he couldn't play without his beloved jersey, jumping up and down and grabbing a ball into his chest in an attempt at trying to convince anyone that would listen that this new top was in no way as velcro-like as his old one. This was the notorious old Broomfield, remember, and there was barely room to swing a cat in the cold, damp, dark and unwelcoming surroundings of the away dressing room.

As ridiculous as it sounds, 'I won't play if I don't

have my jumper', was Budgie's final say on the matter. Miller turned and walked out of the dressing room, muttering, 'well you'll not fuckin' play then' as he left. Back then there was no sub goalie and Jason Gardiner, our youth team keeper, was only there as kit boy. He had never played a first-team game and was likely about to head to the nearest shop for some pre-game munchies when he was summoned to the dressing room. Alex Miller knew he had been backed into a corner, but the manager always has to think of the team first. Going with the rookie against Justin Fashanu and the Beastie Boys would have been like offering up the kid as a sacrificial lamb. Budgie got his way and eventually took his usual place between the sticks.

Regardless of the self-preservation tricks I was learning at the time, I was always a team player and felt everything Budgie did was for Budgie. It was all show and went against the principles I stood for. He made a few more appearances that season, but it was the beginning of the end of his Hibernian career. I liked Budgie, but we were very different football people. He may have been a successful footballer and made a lot more from the game than I did, even winning some trophies, but sometimes morals are worth more than money and medals.

I never won a trophy as a player. Like every young boy who lived to kick a ball about, I grew up dreaming of winning leagues and lifting cups, but it never happened. To some extent I found myself at the right club at the wrong time throughout my career. I hadn't established myself in the first-team squad when Hibs won the League Cup. I was taken to Partick Thistle to help them win the First Division, but the club was very definitely moving in the wrong direction during my time there. Airdrieonians had reached two Scottish Cup finals in the decade before I joined and won the Challenge Cup the year after I left, but my spell was more notable for off-field turmoil. Stranraer was another club to be celebrating almost as soon as I waved goodbye when they clinched the Third Division, ironically against Albion Rovers, who I'd signed for the summer before. Just as the solitary youth cap I picked up while playing for Oxford was the nearest I came to becoming an internationalist, the closest I got to kissing silver came relatively early in my career.

Seasons 1993/94 and 94/95 were the high-watermark of my time at Hibs. I played 65 times in all competitions, including semi-finals of both major trophies and the 1993 League Cup final against Rangers. I was too insecure to ever take my place in the team for granted so as the days ticked down to the final, I was sniffing around desperately for clues as to whether I would be starting or not. Alex Miller was always very cagey so if I was to get a signal either way it would have to be from another source.

In the lead-up to any cup final, there is always a press day where the media are allowed access to anyone they see as having a vital role to play in the game. The captain is always asked for and one or two of the other more high-profile players are generally put up as spokespersons for the club. But the most important thing is that it's ALWAYS players who will start. For

68

fans it's something to look out for, particularly if one of your star players is struggling with injury. The press boys aren't stupid and they know who the fans want to see and who will fill their back pages.

Journeymen midfielders who have fought all their days to establish themselves as a squad player don't make great copy. Reporters all have their friends among players and management and some of the hacks will have been tipped off in advance as to who they might want to interview for an unusual piece in the lead up to the game. And so it was in my case. Ron Scott of the Sunday Post, a giant of a man and a giant among the press corps would surely know what he was doing and would have an inside track. Incredibly, he asked for me so he could take a different angle about the quiet man/hard man, the unsung player in the team and the first thing my fragile, insecure self could think to say was 'Ron, I don't know if I'll be playing'. Even though I'd established myself and was playing fairly well, even though the gaffer had even encouraged me to get an injection to make sure a knee injury wouldn't stop me playing, even that wasn't assurance enough for me.

'David, I'm sure you'll be fine,' was Ron's reply. 'I've spoken to Alex and I reckon you'll be alright. I'm not interviewing someone who'll be sitting on the bench.'

We went through the niceties of the interview and even though Ron, in his calm, inimitable way, had tipped me the wink, it would be the Saturday morning training before I got the nod and could finally believe. Jesus, I was going to play in a cup final, and one taking place at Celtic Park due to rebuilding work

69

at Hampden. Me. I'd been to Celtic Park on hundreds of occasions as a supporter. I'd even played there a couple of times, but now I was to be walking out for a national final. That happened to be against Rangers. You better believe I'd made it. The niggle in my knee had subsided so much that I didn't even have to wear strapping in the final, a rare event indeed.

It wasn't much of a game and the 90 minutes themselves are a bit of a blur. I remember very little apart from the three goals, the winner being Ally McCoist's infamous overhead kick on his return from a five-month layoff due to a leg break which prompted Rangers boss Walter Smith to create his very own piece of history on the back pages with the headline 'Lucky B*****d'. Well he was, wasn't he?

The only other clear memory I have is of Mark Hateley overrunning the ball in the 87th minute and me launching myself into the most ferocious tackle. I clipped the ball and followed through catching him on the knee, hip and cheek. There was a mini melee of sorts with players jostling, shoving and asking the referee to book me. Walter and his assistant Archie Knox were apoplectic, screaming and pointing the finger at me. In injury time Hateley missed a header at the back post when he failed to connect with a perfect, back-post cross and the cameras caught him turning and saying to Richard Gough 'I could see four balls', holding four fingers aloft. It was the legacy of a tackle that would today earn me a high court summons never mind a red card, but in my defence, it wasn't even a foul back in 1993. When I meet Hibs fans now, many of them still ask me about THAT tackle. It seems to have gone down in Hibernian

70

folklore like the Maradona handball has in Argentina (well maybe not, but it's how I like to see it). Was I proud of it? You bet I was. I never had any intention of hurting my opponent. The ball was there to be won and I got it before I got the man. It had been a fairly uneventful final and it had taken me 87 minutes to make my mark in the only way I knew. It was the type of challenge I'd built my fleeting reputation on and if nothing else, it let anyone who was interested know, I would never be messed with, whether it be the first minute or the last.

The aftermath of the League Cup final was strange. The half-hour in the dressing room after the game was purgatory, a crushing low, but it was no worse than a last-minute defeat in a league game when you've worked so hard to get something that your body aches and yet, somehow, it's snatched away from you in injury time. I probably took defeat in a 'normal' game worse than most, but this was a strange experience because that low passed quickly. By the time I went upstairs to meet family and friends in the Players' Lounge, I felt proud to have just played in a cup final. I felt like a fraud somehow as all the stories I'd heard about how devastating it was to lose a final told me I should be feeling much worse. Surely I shouldn't have got over it that quickly? I almost had to put on a 'devastated' face as I greeted everyone with all their sympathetic looks and hugs of comfort. Losing a reserve game hurt me like there'd been a bereavement in the family and yet here I was standing among my teammates and family after a cup final and my overriding feeling was that I'd achieved something. Maybe it was a flaw in my make-up. I wanted to win that final as much as anyone else did but, honestly, at that moment, I wasn't feeling the devastation. We boarded the bus back to Edinburgh and had a pre-booked function at the Hilton to look forward to that evening. It would have been fantastic had it been a winner's party but, nevertheless, we were ordered by Alex Miller to enjoy the occasion and get the loss out of our system but I reckoned I'd done that before I reached the Players' Lounge!

My loving partner Samantha kept my medal in her possession the whole evening, slept with it under her pillow and woke with it in her hand the next morning. Runners-up medal or not, she knew how much that medal meant to me and the sweat, toil and 250 reserve games I'd been through to get it. We made the journey back to Glasgow the next day and stopped in at a cafe in Duke Street for some lunch before heading home. It was while sitting there having my healthy, full Scottish breakfast, I realised I wasn't quite over it yet. A Rangers-supporting local came wandering past with a newspaper under his arm. On recognising me, his paper was no longer a companion but a weapon to bait me with and he proceeded to unroll it to reveal the back page in all its glory. My face open-mouthed in the background, aghast at the sight of McCoist in mid-overhead kick and Walter's infamous words, 'LUCKY B*****D'. It was good-natured banter from someone I knew and had drunk with but it brought it all home in an instant. The devastation and realisation of losing just hit me and I knew then what everyone had been talking about all along. Even though Samantha was sitting there with me I felt completely alone as the horrible emptiness of defeat overcame me.

I was too realistic to console myself with thoughts about there always being a next time. Even then I knew there was a good chance I'd reached my peak and was now in a battle to stay at the top. Well, not THE top, but my top. Achieving doesn't always mean being the best, but it does mean being the best you can be. That's why I don't look back with regret at not having a huge haul of medals to show off. I count myself as immensely lucky to have played for Hibernian, a magnificent club and one of Scotland's biggest. I feel privileged to have played for Partick Thistle, Airdrie, Stranraer, Albion Rovers and, though it was just the once, Clydebank. No one ever paid to see David Farrell, but they did pay to see clubs I played for, clubs that mean an enormous amount to people and their communities. Their numbers might be fewer, but these supporters care just as deeply as the followers of the giants of the game and I hope they appreciate the fact I gave as much for them as I did in the biggest game of my career.

So, no regrets then? Well, only the one.

I'm often asked if, when I see average players these days earning exorbitant amounts of money (and there are plenty of them), I'm jealous or wished I was playing in the current era. The answer to both is no. You can't change the course of your life and, while money might've been a bonus it wouldn't have made me any happier a person. What I would change, if the

73

necessary technology to both travel through time and change a person's genetics existed, would be to have played beyond 34.

I looked after myself throughout my career, but with maturity came fragility. I loved a Saturday night out and rarely missed one, but I was never a mid-week drinker or someone who would over-indulge. My good attitude and application had allowed me to reach a higher level than many players with more ability and the game meant too much to me to put it at risk but, although I didn't realise it at the time, my body was starting to break up from my mid-20s onwards.

I never really saw the warning signs. I was too busy enjoying being a professional footballer. The pain was secondary, but it was almost always there. I'm hardly alone in this. Far better players have had their career curtailed or even ended through injury so I know I'm lucky to have got what I did out of the game. But still... just a couple of years more would have been nice.

I've looked over a lot of old pictures of my playing days and, in almost every one, I'm wearing cycling shorts to protect fraying hamstrings and groins, or a strapping on either knee. Sometimes both. I was plagued with torn hamstrings, medial ligament strains and continual groin problems all through the early 1990s but it was my knees that were the biggest concern. Initially at least.

I had what's scientifically known in football as a niggle in the knee from the start of pre-season training in July 1993. It just wouldn't go away, but I soldiered on for a few months before confiding in our physio

74

Stuart Collie that it was bothering me. I didn't want to tell the manager as, having my usual insecurity about my place in the team, I felt it would give him an opportunity to leave me out and the League Cup semi-final against Dundee United was just round the corner. We discussed the options and it was decided a cortisone injection was the best course of action to reduce the inflammation. We would get the jag done after the Saturday game which would give it a couple of days to settle before the midweek semi-final. I was sitting on the physio's table after the match, anticipating the doctor like a junkie awaiting his fix, when Alex Miller walked in.

'You'll need to get that done now if you want to rest it and be ready for Wednesday,' he boomed.

I looked at Stuart. It was supposed to be our secret and the gaffer wasn't supposed to know. He looked back at me as if to say, 'you didn't expect me not to tell him did you?' He did the right thing by betraying me but it didn't feel like that at the time.

I took many fitness tests over the years, but if ever there was one I wasn't going to fail, it was this one. I hobbled through it with flying colours and, although the knee was nowhere near perfect, it was good enough to allow me to get through the game with the help of strapping that looked like it had been erected by a scaffolder. I played well but, more importantly, Billy McKinlay didn't. 'Badger' was United's main playmaker and throughout the game I chased and harried him to limit his influence on the game, which we won 1-0.

We were in the League Cup Final and I was elated. For someone who'd harboured so many doubts about whether he'd ever be able to call himself a footballer, who had to work to overcome the feeling he shouldn't be mixing in the company he was, who had worked so hard to get to a level other players took for granted, it was a dream come true. Strappings, ice and the cortisone injection were all having the desired effect as the inflammation settled. For the time being anyway.

The knee was playing up again the next season and the groins and hamstrings were tighter than a 10-string banjo, but when I was on the park I felt I was at the pinnacle of my career. A great run in the Scottish Cup saw us face Celtic in the semi-final at Ibrox and, for once, I'd no reason to believe I would be anything other than in the starting line-up. I felt strong and approached the tie at Ibrox with an unusual confidence. Celtic weren't at their best around this time and we genuinely sniffed an opportunity. The game wasn't pretty and that suited me. It was a typically tight, tense semi-final, with chances few and far between and, whilst not being a world beater, I felt I'd done my job. 0-0 and a midweek replay. We prepared as normal and approached the second game just as we had the first, nothing out of the ordinary and no hints as to any changes. I think most people would have assumed we would go into the replay with the same team and play the same way. How wrong I was. Not only did I miss out on the starting XI, but also the bench. I was livid and I genuinely couldn't understand it. I've always been fairly self-critical but I knew I didn't deserve to be dropped and it was from Siberia (metaphorically) that I watched our 3-1 defeat.

I still desperately wanted Hibs to win that game

but even the most hardened of pros with the best attitude would have struggled to suppress a slight feeling of smugness afterwards. There were many times at Hibs when I felt it was easy for me to be made the fall guy and I rarely complained, preferring to take it on the chin and get on with things. On this occasion, however, it stuck in my throat even more when I heard the manager being interviewed after the game.

The commentator had asked the gaffer why he'd changed the team for the replay and, in particular, the reason why I'd been left out. It was an obvious question given the fact we had lost and it seemed, on the face of it, a mistake to change the line-up which had kept us in the tie just a few days previously.

'He was injured,' was Alex Miller's reply.

I was furious. I wasn't injured! I wasn't 100 per cent fit as I'd been covering up frailties in my knee and creaking muscles for five or six years now, but I was as fit as I could be. He'd pulled the classic managerial trick of deflecting rather than publicly admit he MIGHT have made a mistake. I went to see him on the Thursday to ask him why he'd told the press I was injured.

'Because I thought you struggled a bit on Friday and you looked like you were carrying a knock.'

My bravado got the better of me.

'I've been carrying a knock for weeks!'

'Well I was right to leave you out then.'

In football the term 'carrying a knock' doesn't just mean that you've had a kick, it's a general term used for playing with any kind of injury. Managers will use it all the time to let people know a star player is injured without giving away the extent or cause. I assured him I would've contributed just as much as I always had but I'd already incriminated myself and made his point for him.

Despite leaving Alex's office room as I always did, with my head in a spin and feeling like I'd been turned over, I felt it was an admission of guilt on his part that I started the next game. Once again it was at Ibrox and once again and we lost 3-1, with Rangers clinching the League title on this occasion. In nine days we had played in front of 120,000 people at Ibrox. Twice in the home dressing room and once in the away. Unfortunately circumstances would dictate it would be the last time I ever played there.

I missed the first couple of games of the 95/96 season through suspension so my first appearance was to be an attempt to get match-fit in a reserve game at Tannadice. I turned on the turf as a tackle came in from the side and my body weight shifted from one side to the other. When your studs don't shift with it, something has to give. The ligament had come straight off the bone. There was agony for seconds and then nothing. No pain, only numbness which meant I thought I could carry on. I got up, turned and collapsed into a heap, there was nothing there to stop my knee from inverting.

I never even knew I'd dislocated my kneecap until I came back round after the operation. We 'only' thought I'd detached a medial ligament (that's the

78

one on the inside of the knee that stops your leg collapsing inwards) until the surgeon described my knee as having shifted an inch and popping back in before I knew it. Oh, I knew it alright, the pain was excruciating although it only lasted about 10 seconds at the time. It's fair to say I was injured, although it turns out the subsequent dislocation was 'nothing' and it was the medial ligament that was to plague me throughout the rest of my career, along with a left foot of Christy Brown-proportions.

At the time it was to cause me five months of gym work and pain before I could play again. It was only when I came to write this book that I realised how badly that injury had affected my final year as a Hibs player as I only made nine appearances that season. In my time at Hibs I'd played against some of the best players Scottish football had ever seen – Gascoigne, Laudrup, Cooper, McStay, Nicholas and van Hooijdonk. I had fought hard to become a regular but injuries and my never-ending battle to convince the manager that mine wasn't the only name in the hat when it came to who would be left out meant I'd reached a crossroads. Even though I loved playing for that wonderful club on such a fantastic stage it was time to move on.

West End Boy to Beastie Boy
1996-2000

Partick Thistle
Airdrieonians

There are generally three types of transfer in football – the player wants to leave, the club wants the player to leave, or neither wants the player to leave but another club has made it clear they want the player. That said, my move to Partick Thistle came into a fourth category as, even though Hibs had offered me another two-year contract with a small wage rise and a signing-on fee, the terms showed me that Hibs weren't desperate to hold on to me. It's a strange feeling when the club show they still want you by making you an offer, but at the same time you know they wouldn't be too fussed if you left.

Hibs had already shown their hand in that regard. Alex Miller and Dundee United manager Billy Kirkwood had agreed a swap deal, with Brian Welsh and me going in opposite directions. No fees needed to be negotiated and I settled personal terms on a two-year deal with a nice uplift in wages and a signing-on fee. I went into training the next morning fully expecting to be saying my goodbyes, only for Alex to drop the bombshell that the deal was off. I've no way of proving this, but I suspect that Jim McLean, who was now

United chairman, was the one who pulled the plug as revenge for me turning them down eight years previously. Hibs decided to sign big Welshy anyway, pushing my already fragile frame further down the pecking order and proving to me that my future lay elsewhere.

Unlike in 1988, I didn't have offers from two other Premier League clubs to fall back on. I didn't have any, in fact, but I was attracting interest from the other end of Glasgow.

Murdo MacLeod had been an ally at Hibs, pushing me to Alex Miller while he was player/assistant manager and trying to get me in the team. He'd left Hibs to manage Dumbarton and had guided them to promotion before leaving to take over at Partick Thistle. With my aggression and attitude I was Murdo's type of player and he knew I'd be a good influence on other players. Thistle had just become the first team in Scotland to be relegated through the play-off system, with the winning goal scored by the aforementioned Brian Welsh, of all people. Their expectation was to bounce straight back to the Premier League and a deal was done between the clubs to take me and Gareth Evans to Firhill with Ian Cameron going in the opposite direction. The move was the only time in my career a third party helped me negotiate a transfer.

It's a little-known fact, but Steven Gerrard's representative used to do the same job for me. Apparently Stevie introduces him as, 'Struan Marshall, you know, the guy who used to be Davie Farrell's agent.' Struan was my agent for a couple of years and would get me a couple of pairs of Puma King boots every six months. When the Puma Kings became whatever latest promotional model that Greaves Sports couldn't sell, I knew my days of free boots were numbered.

My relationship with Murdo meant no one was really needed to smooth the deal, but I can't complain about the work Struan put in on my behalf and I like to think I helped him on the road to riches. Struan got £500 from me for helping with my transfer from Hibs to Partick. It wouldn't surprise me if he got £500,000 from LA Galaxy for facilitating Gerrard's move to the States.

The postscript to my links to Steven Gerrard is that I later discovered that Gareth was getting £50 more than me at Firhill. I hope for Stevie G's sake he's never suffered the same fate but, even if he has, at least he's got a few medals to pawn if things get tight.

In the shady world of football transfers things aren't always what they first appear to be, as I was to learn when I arrived at Firhill and was told that I was five years late. It transpired that Jim Mclean wasn't the only manager to play personal politics and that Alex Miller and John Lambie were at it as well. In between my second and third contracts, I spent a year signing month-to-month deals. While football was never about money for me, it didn't mean I would let myself be taken for a ride. I'd a good idea what others at the club were earning and thought I'd done enough to merit more than the £30 a week pay rise and £1000 signing-on fee I was being offered.

In the days before the Bosman ruling, the power remained with the club so it was highly unlikely I would be able to leave unless Hibs were willing to let me go for next to nothing and, as I'd yet to fully establish myself in the first-team, it was unlikely many cash offers would be coming in. Eventually I was called into Alex Miller's office to be told Portadown had agreed to pay a nominal fee for me and if I wanted, I could go over to Northern Ireland for a few days for a look at the set-up.

This was the height of 'The Troubles' and Portadown was a staunchly Protestant area, which instantly made me nervous. I went over to assess it, even though I didn't see it as a particularly good career move. Irish football was a backwater and it was only older pros from Scotland in the twilight of their careers who no longer had any offers in this country that had gone there for a final payday. Because that was it you see, the money on offer was good by 1991 standards. £300 per week and a £10,000 signing-on fee was much, much more than I was being offered by Hibs. They wanted me to sign a two-year deal and move over there. There were already Scottish guys in Ireland, but they were flying out on a Friday night, playing on a Saturday and flying straight home. This was something they were clearly trying to get away from and I really wasn't sure if I wanted to be their guinea pig. Secondly, and this was key, I knew that, as a Catholic, I'd have to be careful where I ate, drank and ventured to at the weekend. As well as that I had the short hair, peely-wally skin and Scottish accent that could've seen me mistaken for an off-duty British Army recruit. It was like being called both an orange and fenian bastard all over again, but with real danger this time. I didn't fancy being a sitting duck for both sets of bounty hunters and thought I'd have to walk about in a balaclava to protect my identity... though on second thoughts, that wasn't such a great idea either!

There was a significant police presence when I arrived at Belfast Airport and headed off in search of a cab. They weren't there for me, of course, but to try and decrease tension after a recent car bomb attack had killed the driver and passenger of another taxi. That, my friends, was the final nail in the coffin and I'd made my mind up before I even reached the old-fashioned, ramshackle ground that this wasn't for me. The staff and players at Portadown gave me a fantastic welcome as, in their eyes I was to be a marquee signing, but they weren't to know my mindset. As I went through the motions of playing a practice game I was already back at Easter Road, fighting for my place and my future.

What I wasn't to discover until I arrived at Firhill was that former Thistle boss John Lambie had been an admirer of my 'combative' style and had tried to sign me from Hibs previously. Alex Miller's dislike for Lambie and a fear that letting a player go to another Premier League team might come back to haunt him scuppered any chance of a deal. I was told that at this point Lambie hatched a plan that the Portadown manager Ronnie McFall, one of his closest friends, would sign me. Then, after a few months, Thistle would come in for me and repay any money dished out by the Northern Irish outfit.

This would have been the perfect scenario for me, two signing-on fees, a wage rise and a return to Glasgow and the Premier League within a few months. The only problem with this plan, of course was that no one had bothered to tell ME. Footballers are very often the last people to know in football.

87

*

I loved Firhill and settled very quickly. All of a sudden I was a bigger fish in a smaller pond. Players were looking up to me and the young lads would seek my advice. I genuinely wanted to help them if I could, but I also wanted to show the powers-that-be that I was a good influence and not a jumped-up prima donna who had come from a bigger club to swan about. Within a few weeks I felt as though I was going to spend the rest of my career at Firhill. Murdo made me captain and I took all of the duties that came with it in my stride.

I played the first four games of the new season in midfield, but it quickly became apparent, with the cuts being made to the playing staff and general running costs associated with relegation to the lower division, it was unlikely promotion would be possible. We struggled to string results together and, by the end of the fifth game of the season, my form hadn't been great either so I went to see Murdo. I'd assessed the League and the standards and, although I wasn't playing well, I knew I was better than what I was alongside and against. I wanted to play in my best position, centre-back. Thankfully Murdo agreed and I slotted in there for the next few games. It was a canter. I'd found my level at last and as well as being comfortable with the club off the pitch, I was now very happy on it.

This was a rare example of a visit to the manager's office bringing about a mutually satisfactory outcome. Don't believe all those stories you read about players battering down the manager's door because

88

they're not playing. I don't know what it's like in the real working world going to see your manager, but in a football sense it's very intimidating. You wait like a naughty schoolboy outside the headmaster's office, ear at the door for the conversation between the gaffer and his assistant to pause. You then knock as politely as you can, half-hoping the gaffer hasn't heard it and the whole sorry confrontation can be avoided. What happens next can vary, but, in my experience, the assistant manager is often asked to stay as an ally to the boss, usually as a witness, and occasionally as a peacemaker. I went to see every manager I ever played under throughout my career and, almost every time I went out feeling worse than I did when I went in. There are bog-standard replies to the immortal 'why am I not playing?' question that I asked of many managers on many occasions.

'You're doing well, just keep working hard and you'll get back in.'

Which actually means 'you've been shit and it'll be a miracle if you play again before Christmas.'

'It's horses for courses, you didn't play this week but you might play next week.'

Actually means 'Now that you've lost your place, you'll struggle to get it back.'

'You've still got a future at the club.'

Actually means 'Don't bother coming to see me when your contract's up. You're getting freed'.

And that was it. Back out the door after the character assassination, tail between legs and scratching your head, wondering what had just happened. You've just been 'gaffered'. They don't teach it on the coaching courses, but it must have been the same when they played. How else can it be explained that they have all learned to do it exactly the same way?

Anyway, things worked out better than I expected when I made my unannounced visit to Murdo's office. Although I had a reputation in the Premier League for being a bit of a clogger, I began to show what I'd suspected all along – that I was actually better than I was given credit for at times and could play a bit.

The only problem was that, although my own form was very good, those cutbacks to the squad had taken their toll and we were no better than a mid-table outfit. It was disappointing as I'd dreamt of taking them back to the Premier League, but the lack of investment both on and off the pitch, coupled with the financial implications of relegation from the Premier League, were now pushing the club towards financial meltdown. The season was a disaster as we finished 6th in the league.

I managed to win the two Player of the Year trophies that were on offer. It's amazing the difference in mentality you have when you become a first choice at a football club. I'd spent eight seasons at Hibs struggling with myself and fighting to become a first-team regular. I lost count of the number of times I played and trained with injuries that would have sent most people to the treatment table. I got as many injuries in training as I did in games because I always felt if I missed a day, the manager could see it as an opportunity to leave me out. In reality I was putting myself out of contention for even longer as a minor niggle, which should have been protected, was aggravated into a strain. As a first choice, I was actually able to play in many more games as I'd no issue with sitting out the odd day's training because of a bit of muscle tightness as I KNEW I'd be playing on the Saturday.

I could honestly see a career progression at that time where I would move into coaching at the club and then take over as manager. The fans liked me too, and, with the ground being just 15 minutes from my flat in Dennistoun, it was like a home from home. Maryhill was mine.

For those that don't know the place, Maryhill is in a quiet suburb in the West End of Glasgow, otherwise known as bandit country. At Hibs we had our regular training ground and we knew where we would train every day, but it was a different situation at Thistle. We'd be on public parks most of the time, and some weeks we trained at three or four different facilities. Given the financial difficulties the club was starting to experience, that may partly have been down to bills not being paid and us having to shift from one location to another before we were caught and invoiced. It was training ground roulette. One of our more regular destinations was the Firhill complex, a 3G surface right in the middle of the Bronx. We were training there at around 11am one day when one of our balls flew over the fence that enclosed the astroturf. A young gentleman (all of 14) who just happened to be of a mind that school was something you opted into, grabbed the errant ball and did a runner with it.

I never gave it a second thought and instinctively

91

clambered up the fence behind the goal to give chase. This was a nearly new Mitre Delta match ball, a prize worth risking my neck for and no doubt the reason why Maryhill's very own Robin Hood was now making his way through the scheme with it under his arm. At the top of the fence (probably 40ft) it didn't seem such a great idea, but I couldn't help myself. I'm a fully paid up member of the red ash pitch crew and the rule book clearly states: nobody steals your ball. I threw myself over the other side and ran onto the road. My studs weren't great for grip as we dodged through parked cars and onto the main road but I felt like I had him as, even though I wasn't the quickest, the gap between me and the fugitive was closing. He jinked up a tenement close and, unless he knew a way through the back gardens, he was mine. First floor, second floor, top floor and there he was, standing triumphantly with the shiny football under his arm and the other hand on the letterbox. I hadn't noticed any barking until this point, but now that I had, I swear that dog had a megaphone. It may well have been a Jack Russell, but there seemed just as much chance it was a Rottweiler, Bull Terrier, Staffie or whatever other housing scheme status symbol was 'in' at the time. He was teasing me now.

'If ah chap this letterbox an' the dug opens the door, he'll huv you!'

Jesus, I thought. Not only is this dog a ferocious predator, it can open doors itself! At this point, whilst that Mitre Delta had become very important to me, a greater priority was still having my testicles attached to my body by the time I returned to training. I reluctantly accepted defeat. Six months previously I'd

92

played at Ibrox in front of 50,000 people and here I was, slinking my way back down the stairs with that unmistakeable sound of stud on concrete echoing in the close after chasing the local ned through the streets for a training ball. At least MY balls were still intact but the slagging I took from my teammates was emasculating enough in itself.

Two days later my adversary walked straight into Jaconelli's cafe where we all ate our lunch with the Mitre Delta still proudly displayed under his arm. This time there was no escape and, as if to mock my Krypton Factor-esque approach to getting the ball back, my teammate Billy MacDonald simply walked up to him and put his hand out, saying, 'Geez it ya wee dick'. It was over and the Mitre was property of Partick Thistle Football Club once again.

It's fair to say that I was never a goalscorer. My job was generally to prevent them, but I did manage to hit the back of the net 10 times in my career. Two of them, my only strikes for Hibs in fact, came within a few, goal-den weeks in January 1994 when I briefly threatened to become prolific.

I'll tell you what though, if Thistle had drawn Hibs in the cup during my time there and I had managed to find myself on the scoresheet, there's no question that I would have celebrated. Same if I came up against any of my old clubs at any point during my career. I can't stand the current trend for players shrugging apologetically when they score against their former club. If the situation had arisen then I wouldn't have

93

gone over the top, particularly if I was right in front of the busiest part of the opposition fans, but, at the same time, that goal may have helped my current team secure a win or a point. I would have been more desperate than ever to do well and show my former employers what they were missing so I would have been delighted and wouldn't have bothered trying to hide that fact. I find it almost disrespectful that players DON'T celebrate. It's a fad players have picked up on after seeing someone high-profile do it on Match of the Day, and it's typical of some of the guff that players use to pander to supporters these days.

I like to think I generally had a good relationship with the fans of the clubs I played for. They could see I gave them my all and I would take time to attend functions and speak to them if we met off the pitch. I enjoyed that side of the job and certainly respected the fact the supporters were paying to see the team they loved every Saturday, but not once during my 18-year career did I ever go out to win a match for them.

Footballers are selfish and, as I said previously, they're generally motivated by one of two things – winning football matches or the financial bonus that comes with it – so take it with a pinch of salt next time your star man says the team are going to do it for the fans.

As a player, the difference that a big, vocal support can make to you on the park is incredible but, equally, if the fans are getting on the back of a particular player or the whole team, then the booing is 100 per cent counter-productive. Players, too, can galvanise the support. I've seen games turn on aggressive tackles that won nothing more than a a throw-in deep in your own half but got previously critical fans out of their seats roaring in appreciation.

Players and fans are working towards the same goal and can ultimately celebrate together but, as for the men on the park doing it for the punters in the crowd, forget it. It's just something players say.

I remember an incident early on in my career that was a petty and naive attempt to get into the fans' good books. As a young player of around 22 I took part in an 'A to Z'-type profile in the Hibs programme. One of the questions asked was 'Favourite Song'. It hadn't been long since Hibs had won the League Cup and, as it was a favourite of the punters at the time, I chose 'No Cups in Gorgie'. I got lots of nice letters from Hibs fans saying how much they enjoyed my comments, but among them was a slightly larger, padded package. My immediate thought was that one of the boys had shoved a pair of knickers in an envelope in the hope I would fall for it and brag around the dressing room. However, on opening the package, I found a photocopy of my article, on which some Hearts fans had scrawled a beautiful, heartfelt message. They had also enclosed another, less kindly smelling 'message'. I found it funny and strangely flattering that the Jambos had gone to that effort given I was only a fringe player at the time but it also taught me that the more you open your mouth, the more likely you are to have it shut for you.

Unfortunately, I never quite managed to learn that lesson about keeping my mouth shut in mind and it was to be this, along with another genuine attempt to connect with supporters, that was to bring my time at Firhill to an end.

*

Even after such a disappointing season I still felt I had a long term future at the club and the career path I'd decided upon meant I was under an obligation to continue to push everyone forward for the cause. That was all to change after the last game of the season when Murdo was sacked and it became clear how grim the financial situation was. I called the chairman Jim Oliver personally as I felt I had a duty to the manager who had signed me, and also as captain of the club, to express my opinion. In truth, based purely on results, Murdo had deserved to be relieved of his duties, but I felt there had been mitigating circumstances which should have afforded him the grace of a few months at the start of the following season. Jim was having none of it and, having gotten rid of the manager, he was also intent on getting rid of the club. He no longer wanted to own Thistle and was adamant he could no longer subsidise it either. It was the start of a process which would, six months later, see me leave the club in acrimonious circumstances.

Gordon Chisholm was put in interim charge for pre-season, but the squad had been decimated and there were only a few senior players left, alongside some kids. I felt the players should show a united front behind Chissy for the sake of the club but there was also the possibility that, were he to be given the job, there may have been a chance of stepping up to that player/coach role I was now longing for. The selfishness always creeps in somewhere. It was important to keep the players' spirits up and make sure we applied

96

ourselves well as concerns about money troubles continued and the squad was depleted further.

At this point two things happened. The fans decided to mount a campaign called 'Save the Jags' and the club appointed John McVeigh as manager. Staff were being laid off at the club and rumours of impending bankruptcy meant the big, happy family club I joined had become a skeleton in just over a year. We had to start washing our own training kit and the new manager's methods were questioned by players and staff alike. John had been assistant manager at Airdrie, who had achieved success with a team of players who were established and moulded into a certain way of training and way of playing; the Airdrie way. Like Mark Lawrenson, John didn't appreciate that this couldn't be instantly applied at a club with players unsuited to that style.

We started the season poorly and quickly became embroiled in a relegation battle. By now, the Save the Jags campaign was in full swing with bucket collections and all sorts of fundraising events to ensure wages would be paid and the club could continue to fulfil its fixtures. The Partick Thistle I loved was now a shadow club, not only off the pitch but also on it as the manager tried to turn us into Airdrie. There was as much chance of turning us into Bayern Munich. We didn't have the players to play that way and by the time we had reached the quarter-point of the season, very few players had the inclination to try to adapt. I was doing my best to continue rallying and leading the group, but the truth was we were sinking, not just as a team, but as a club.

The manager's answer was to question our fitness.

I couldn't believe it. We couldn't pass the ball from A to B, had no discernible team shape and we were defending like schoolgirls and the answer was to run the bollocks off us three days a week and have a game of five-a-sides and work on some set pieces on a Friday. I went to see the manager to express my concern that some of his methods weren't working and that some of the players were scared of making a mistake and scared of the manager. In football, respect for a manager is one thing, but fear is another. Very few players ever play to their potential if they fear their manager. John was a very strong, aggressive and forceful guy and, while his methods may well have worked at Airdrie, I felt it was having a negative effect on some players. It wouldn't have been the first time I saw players destroyed by the fear of making a mistake. They retreat so far into their shell that they don't actually do anything at all. Unfortunately for me, having the club's best interests at heart backfired spectacularly as it was decided that not only was I being a troublemaker, I was the instigator of the unrest.

I was called into the manager's office a few days later and told that it was nothing to do with the conversation we had only a couple of days earlier, but I was being stripped of the captaincy. It was clear I was being made an example of to the rest of the players and, as a popular figure at the club, it was also clear I was an easy target. John felt his position was threatened by my presence in the dressing room and, as manager, he had the right to load whatever bullets he wanted under the circumstances. But he was firing at the wrong target. I took my medicine like a man and vowed to dig in and show him he'd made a mistake.

Meanwhile, the campaign to save the club had gathered pace and I felt it was the perfect chance to demonstrate the players' camaraderie and to thank the fans for their efforts. There was no pandering to the fanbase here. The club these guys loved was in danger of going under and their efforts were the only thing ensuring we got paid every week. They deserved to know we were willing to do our bit.

I organised for the local paper to come along and do a piece with players pleading for more investment to pull the club through the uncertain times. Results were poor and I felt it might be something that would not only galvanise fundraising efforts but would also have a positive effect on the park. The Evening Times ran the story on the back page, and in it I said that, even though the fans had proved the club was worth saving, its financial plight was so great that they couldn't keep it alive themselves.

My unilateral PR campaign didn't go down well with the manager and, with more stories coming from the dressing room about players being unhappy with training, a meeting was called. One by one, the squad were asked if they were happy and one by one they mumbled 'yeah', 'kinda' or 'I just think we need to work harder'. I was astonished. When my turn came I explained, as I had in his office, that I felt we should be working on tactics and ball retention rather than running three days a week.

And then the backlash came. John turned to his assistant Peter Hetherston and said, 'See, I told you it was him'. I was dismayed that only two players, Gregg Watson and Iain Nicholson, had offered any kind of resistance. Right there and then I knew that team was doomed to relegation as they were scared of the manager.

Afterwards I was called to his office and told in no uncertain terms that I'd undermined the whole Save the Jags campaign by saying the fans couldn't save the club. It was nonsense, of course, and the real reason I was being punished was for daring to disagree with the gaffer. I was ordered to train on my own away from the rest of the first-team squad and told I would never play for the club again. I knew this wasn't the board's thinking as the chairman quickly stepped in and asked me what had happened for our relationship to have broken down so badly. I kept my dignity and told him he'd need to see the manager for an explanation. I was still owed a £5000 signing-on fee and needed to do everything by the book to ensure the club couldn't force me out the door without paying me what I was due.

I had hoped for more support from the players, but understood their reticence as they feared the manager and had their own contracts to protect. I was banned from the home dressing room and, when I turned up for the away game at Cappielow on the Saturday, I was turned away from the team bus and made to train on my own inside the stand. As I ran up and down the stairs of the stadium, it was the one and only time in my whole career when I wished that the team I played for would be beaten. I loved the club but the disrespect I now had for the manager was so great I was prepared to commit the ultimate treason. But, as a person, I was never going to be beaten.

I was forced to do the equivalent of a week's preseason training on my own. It was torture, but the

100

more I ran and the more pain I was going through, the more it strengthened my resolve to hang in there. The manager was trying to break me in the hope that I would walk away and save the club from paying up the rest of my contract, but there was no way that was going to happen.

The team lost their next two games — no surprise as we had already been on a poor run — before I was called back to the manager's office and told I was back in the squad for Saturday's game at Falkirk. We barely spoke a word to each other until I was walking out onto the pitch. John came over and whispered 'don't do it for me, do it for yourself' in my ear. I looked at him and laughed. We both knew that the relationship had disintegrated into nothing and he was just getting his final little dig in. We won the match 1-0, but it was to be my last game for the club.

My release was negotiated the next week and I received a lovely call from the Thistle chairman at the time expressing his gratitude and wishing me luck. I had agreed that what I was owed could be paid in instalments to help the club stabilise, but he insisted on paying me in full as soon as the club were back on an even keel, which was a real credit to him. Thankfully, in the coming weeks the Jags were saved, but I couldn't spend too much time thinking about them or dwelling on what had gone on. I was an Airdrieonians player now.

The end to my time at Firhill was disappointing, but I was learning more and more that's what happens in football. You've overstayed your welcome at a club and you move on. Whether it's on your terms or not, you quickly realise that clubs care very little for you and that, ultimately, you're nothing more than a commodity for trading or discarding when your time is up. It's one of the reasons why footballers rarely remain close friends with other players. Most players are too afraid to get too close to anyone as they know that if they don't move on themselves, others certainly will. Whilst at a club your commitment to that team and its players is absolute, but they're only short-term acquaintances. You recognise that you're unlikely to be at any particular club for the long term and, as such, the odd phone call back and forth on departure is usually enough to satisfy the emotional shortfall before you move onto the next group of players. Your teammates become your best pals socially for a short time, but one or the other moves on and that's it. Of the hundreds of players and coaches I've worked with there are only four or five who I consider to be close friends. I've got lots of pals in the game among past players and coaches, but when you leave a club, it's very rare to take many real, close friends with you.

But I was leaving Maryhill and it was time to build all those dressing-room relationships again. My destination was somewhat ironic given John McVeigh's obsession with trying to turn Thistle into Airdrie, but my new manager Alex 'Doddie' MacDonald had built his team over several years. He only signed a certain type of player, one who he felt could fit in to the 'Beastie Boys' ethos and siege mentality. The nickname was nothing to do with hip-hop – everything they did oozed nastiness and the team's spirit was built around revelling in the 'no one likes us, we don't care' attitude.

I could be that guy on the pitch without a problem, but off it there were a few things I had to be wary of. When you first go into a new club, the current players resent anyone being too loud and overbearing or too cocky and full of themselves. I wasn't any of those things, but I was still slightly uncomfortable as I entered that cauldron in the first few days.

First of all, the place was full of ex-Jambos – Jimmy Sandison, Kenny Black, Walter Kidd and Gary Mackay were all part of the Airdrie dressing room now. I was more than aware that I wasn't particularly liked on the pitch at the best of times and had gone hammer and tongs with these guys in Edinburgh derbies. I knew I was likely to have a few barriers to break down, although when people met me socially and I'd behave like a Mormon on a bonus they were always surprised by how different I was to that guy who charged about the pitch.

Secondly, Kenny Black had broken my rib only a year or so earlier in a game at Firhill. As I jumped for a header, Blackie did the old pro's trick and allowed me to jump first, giving him the chance to have a wee dig at my side. I tried to play on but could hardly breathe and had to come off and was out of action for another six weeks. That in itself wasn't an issue for me, if I was to give it out then I certainly couldn't moan about having to take one now and again. When I bumped into Blackie a few months later at the SPFA Player of the Year dinner, I went over to tell him so. It was almost an appreciation of the fact he'd 'done' me, from one warrior to another, but, with everyone fairly well oiled, it turned into a minor slagging match between me and a few of the Airdrie lads. Neither Blackie or myself was particularly aggressive off the park so we parted with a handshake and red faces. I was embarrassed there had even been raised voices and felt it was important I wipe the slate clean with Kenny on my first day at training.

'Blackie, you know how you broke my rib and we had that stupid argument after the PFA dinner? Well just to say, it's not an issue for me. We're all in it together now.'

'Faz, I don't know what the fuck you're talking about. Welcome to Airdrie.'

There were no initiations at Airdrie, no easy way in. No singing competitions (many a young player's career path has been mapped out by a desperately inept version of Deacon Blue's 'Dignity'), or 'naked laps'. You had to be accepted the hard way, as yourself. Whether Kenny had remembered either incident or not, he was completely dismissive of any notion that there was history between us and I'm fortunate that he became one of my closest confidantes in the battle to win the other players over. His attitude and commitment typified the Airdrie of that era and he remains one of the very few people from within the game to whom I'm still fairly close today.

Dressing rooms are ruthless, macho places and you need to be strong to survive in that environment. One of the things that the Airdrie of the 1990s is known for is being one of the clubs that Justin Fashanu — the first high-profile, openly gay footballer — played for. When I played against him for Hibs, Fash's stature and power were what concerned me, not his

104

sexuality. It was also a far bigger deal for the media than it ever was for his teammates at Airdrie, many of whom were still there when I joined four years later and who couldn't have cared less about him being gay so long as he could be relied on when he stepped onto the park.

When it comes down to it, there are only two things you need to prove in order to ingratiate yourself to a new dressing room. One is your ability as a player and the other is how you are as a person. That's all your teammates will judge you on: not your religion, nationality, race or anything else. Footballers aren't naturally more virtuous than anyone in any other aspect of life, but, by the same token, we're not the ignorant knuckle-dragging Neanderthals we're often made out to be either. The banter is unforgiving but rarely, if ever, does it tip over into bullying and every single person who walks into a dressing room has the opportunity to earn the respect of their colleagues on the basis of nothing more than their abilities and the content of their character. And in that regard we're ahead of many more PC industries where tokenism is mistaken for equality.

As a player I had no problems. Airdrie were in the First Division at that time and I'd shown at Thistle that I was comfortable at that level. I knew the players could see that and would know me well enough to see that I would run through a brick wall for them. I was the type of player who would thrive at Airdrie, the winner who would support his teammates and stop at nothing to win.

My first game was away at Falkirk and I was on the bench. We came in at half-time a goal down, but we had been awful. Doddie launched into the team, his face red and twisted with anger, as they hadn't worked hard enough and that was a cardinal sin for the man. A tray of cups went flying in the direction of Stevie Cooper. In response Stevie, who was no shrinking violet himself, picked up a flip-flop and threw it, not at the manager, but just anywhere to demonstrate his own anger. It hit the wall just above my head, but he was saying sorry to the manager before it had even left his hand. I glanced up at Alex and he looked at me as if to say 'don't even think about opening your mouth'. I said nothing, which was unusual for me, but in my head I was thinking 'I'm going to like it here'.

Spirit was the thing that Alex's Airdrie had been built on and the bond was unbreakable. It had been nurtured over a number of years and strengthened by keeping hold of a hard core of players who bought into his philosophy. It made bedding new players into the team a much easier task.

Different managers will have different ideas on how you should play and how you should train. The two I worked for the longest had played for the same manager – Jock Wallace – for years and yet their approaches to the game were at opposite ends of the spectrum. Alex Miller was a thorough coach and an excellent tactician. He and Alex MacDonald were so different that I doubt they would have got on, despite playing so many games together.

We were very well organised at Hibs and knew exactly where we should be on the pitch. We were

106

drilled and disciplined and that came from many hours of what is commonly known as 'shape'. This means setting up your formation (4-4-2 in this case) against the reserves, running through repetition after repetition of what would happen at certain times on the pitch, and endless drills of where each player should be. I loved it, but it meant that when I came to Airdrie I had to adapt to a different way of training and a different tactical approach to the game. Many players resented shape and got bored, but it made that Hibs side a better team and much more difficult to beat. Players who don't buy into it tend to be the ones whose attitude to training isn't great anyway. There are also drills when you set up without any opponents and work through where you should be in relation to where the ball is and how you can position yourself to avert danger. At Hibs we would be so well drilled we knew where each player would be should a certain scenario develop.

Alex Miller was years ahead of his time when it came to preparation. We were working with esteemed sports scientist Brian Ewing way back then and his ideas and developments were implemented to the letter. Blood testing, aerobics, swimfit sessions, fitness testing and weights sessions were all integrated into our training programme. This was 20 years ago don't forget; some clubs don't even do that now.

We trained hard, and we made the best of what we had. And we didn't do too badly on the back of it. It was intense, physical training, lots of small sided games at a high tempo, 'match' tempo. We did double sessions – virtually unheard of at the time – where we would work on our shape in the afternoon. If Alex

MacDonald had watched us train and seen us with all our fancy heart monitors and blood testing, he'd have told his Airdrie players that he'd just watched a team of namby pambies being pampered to within an inch of their lives, and that they would never match the physical approach (a nice way to put it) of his Beastie Boys.

Miller wasn't always popular with the players. He was a disciplined man and some players can't work with that level of intensity, but his record at Hibs and subsequent coaching career shows that a lack of popularity doesn't always equate to a lack of success. Not being popular among the players was certainly not an accusation you could level at his former teammate.

Alex MacDonald was a magnificent man. A leader who had won everything possible with Rangers, his 5' 5" frame belied the desire and toughness of the man. It was a privilege to play for him. My football allegiances were entirely different to his and there were times when he wouldn't let you forget it. Political correctness wasn't a concept Doddie was very familiar with. My first meeting with him was in the office of club chairman George Peat to agree personal terms. He asked me what team I supported. I knew he'd know already but instinctively said 'Celtic'.

'Is the ink dry on that contract yet George?'

It was his way of letting me know that I would be welcome into the Airdrie fold, regardless of what I was. He was never slow to greet you with a wee wink or a whistle of The Sash as he passed you in the corridor in the wake of an Old Firm game that had gone in his favour. I never did dare to reciprocate with The Soldier's Song if the result ever went my way!

He didn't coach in the most literal sense. MacDonald was a 'man manager'. His philosophy was that if you were playing against someone, then you had to be better than them, one-versus-one. Not necessarily a better player, but for that 90 minutes, you had to be BETTER than your opponent. They weren't to play, but you were. You had to run faster, fight harder, be stronger and as long as you gave your all, his backing was unswerving. We had good players at the time, often much better than they were given credit for, but nothing typified the Alex MacDonald way more than a squad of footballers who would have run through a brick wall for him. He'd an eye for that type of player, you know, the one that everyone hated playing against.

At Airdrie we hardly trained. Contrary to what I was used to at Hibs, there was no emphasis on sports science and certainly very little shape done. Yet everyone knew where they should be and what their responsibilities were. It was a simple philosophy – if the guy nearest you scored it was your fault. If you weren't marking someone, you'd better do it quick or you'd be on the end of Doddie's red-faced 'hairdryer'. And if you still didn't do it, you didn't play. Simple. As long as we worked as hard as we could, we would get Sunday and Monday off. The Monday incentive was really a consequence of the wee man's penchant for visiting the Rob Roy Social Club on a Sunday, but his players had so much respect for him he could've turned up for the first time on a Friday and still no one would have cared.

Tuesday was a running day, where we did all our fitness work. We'd start with a 30-minute 'fartlek', a physically demanding run where the pace, as dictated by fitness fanatic Kenny Black, went up and down in periods varying from 10 seconds to a minute. Fartlek is Swedish for 'speed play' so, contrary to popular football belief, the run wasn't so named because it made you breathe out of your arse. After that it was four sets of 60-yard runs, 16 in total. Flat out. And the 'pièce de résistance', eight half laps of the pitch. A brutal, physical day, but eased with knowledge that we had Wednesday off to recover. That's right, we didn't get a sniff of the ball until Thursday when we played small-sided games and enjoyed some finishing and shooting practice. Friday was a short morning where we'd have a team briefing and a quick rundown of our opponents, a few short sprints and a 15 minute five-a-side. We were a full-time club training part-time, but we worked harder in those few hours than some clubs did in double the amount of time. The respect we had for the manager was absolute and what was about to happen to him was an absolute disgrace.

If someone was to slam the door of their club in my face to prevent them catching whatever it was I carried around with me, I couldn't blame them. I've been something of a Jonah figure throughout my career. Most of the clubs I've been at suffered serious threats to their future during or after my time with them. Oxford were to fall down the divisions and out of the Football League altogether. The fans were forced to mount a 'Hands Off Hibs' campaign to fend off an attempted takeover by Hearts during

110

my time at Easter Road and I've already covered the Save the Jags story. Clyde somehow limp along year after year while Dundee were to plunge into a second administration not long after I left and Notts County's problems appear to be ongoing. Celtic Nation have ceased to exist altogether and the current incarnations of Gretna and Clydebank are in the Junior and non-league ranks respectively. Most of these problems can be traced to boardroom ineptitude and arrogance, and that was certainly the case at Airdrie.

The club was not in a good way when I arrived. The glory days of the previous decade were now a fading memory but, worse still, the club was losing its identity. After selling the notorious Broomfield, Airdrie had opted to share Cumbernauld's Broad-wood stadium with Clyde for an indefinite period. As is often the case in these situations, the fans never followed. Airdrie were built on the nastiness that purveyed every square inch of the old Broomfield, the ramshackle stand and poisonous atmosphere that destroyed many an opposition's prima donna before they had even reached the pitch. Unfortunately the supporters who also revelled in their intimidating reputation were no longer following the club to its temporary home. It was the beginning of a long spiral that would ultimately result in the ignominy of liqui-dation and significant human cost.

The new ground was finally being built in Airdrie to replace the old Broomfield, but, having taken so long to come to fruition, The Shyberry Excelsior Sta-dium (a mistake of huge proportions not to name it New Broomfield) became more of a white elephant than a shiny new home.

Initially, things seemed to go well. I was keeping reasonably fit, although I was now in a position where I couldn't play without the protection of insulated cycling shorts which were so heavy that running felt more like treading water at times. We were hovering around the middle of the First Division, which was a little below the expectations of a club who had been used to Premier League football and cup final appearances only a few years previously, but there were highlights in that initial period as well. We beat Celtic 1-0 in the League Cup quarter final in front of a capacity crowd but, by the time we returned to the stadium for a home game the following Saturday, the crowd had again dwindled to what was becoming an unsustainable level. We had lost the fans. They had stopped going when the club lost its identity and moved to Cumbernauld and, until we were challenging at the top of the First Division, they wouldn't be back.

Results continued to be inconsistent and the board, in all their wisdom, decided to sack Alex MacDonald. It was a disgraceful decision given the service he'd given the club, but no manager is ever given any grace when the board starts getting grief from disgruntled punters. It's the same wherever you go in football. Chairmen and directors are generally successful businessmen and when they sit on panels and committees in their own workplace they're the top men. Rarely does anyone ever say 'no' or show them any dissent. So when fans turn to vent their anger at THEM on a Saturday, they don't like it. Screaming fans, faces twisted in frustration telling them where to go and threatening boycotts isn't something they like or are geared up to deal with. So as a fan, if you ever

112

want a manager sacked, direct your anger directly at the board while they're sitting on their comfy seats on a Saturday. You'll soon get your wish.

When it comes to that point there's only one way they can make it stop and that's with the inevitable 'mutual consent' announcement. Alex MacDonald would never have allowed them the pleasure of a parting that could be construed as mutual. He was too proud. He told us he was plain-and-simple sacked as he toured the dressing room, shaking everyone's hand and wishing us luck. A numbness came over the entire room. Alex MacDonald WAS Airdrie and he was reduced to this, the briefest one-minute cameo before heading out of the door for the last time. He was as close to tears as any man could be, but he would never break down, he wouldn't allow us to see that. Not that man. His parting shot was tell us that he was 'sorry at the way things are going to work out'. He clearly had an idea of what was to come at the club although, being the manager he was, he'd protected us from any of the rumours about impending financial doom to that point.

I felt a strong sense of loyalty to Alex and, after the game, I gathered the players and we decided to write a letter addressed to the chairman and the board, expressing our disgust at the decision to relieve Doddie of his duties. In truth it was a pointless exercise as the board were never likely to change their mind and it was even less likely that the wee man would have come back if they had, but we felt it was important to at least make our feelings known. The chairman came to speak to us on the Monday and explained to us that whilst he respected our opinion and understood our reasons for writing the letter, the decision had been made.

Gary Mackay took over as he'd been the most senior player in the dressing room, and we played out the rest of the season with a mediocrity that was to typify the current status of the club. I was pleased Gary got the job and I was happy to be offered a new contract; despite the club making it clear that, due to cutbacks, no-one who re-signed would receive a signing-on fee. I got a wage rise instead which meant I was now earning more than I had when I was in the Premier League. This should have allowed the club to budget over the course of the season comfortably, but with crowds dwindling further and debts rising due to the length of time it took to build the stadium and the ridiculous overheads associated with it, serious cash flow problems quickly surfaced.

On a personal note, I'd started my second full season at Airdrie fairly well, keeping relatively fit. That's the thing about football – 'relatively fit' becomes the norm because, once the season starts, it's rare that you will play a game at 100 per cent, even though you are at your strongest physically. There's always something niggling: a pain, an ache, a piece of you that needs to be strapped up and protected. I was at the stage where I was either recovering from one injury or just about to have another. It was clear my knee was never going anywhere near that magical 100 per cent ever again.

I was able to make accommodations by changing

my running style slightly, but this was throwing my body alignment out of kilter, making my back muscles spasm and causing already fragile hamstrings and groins to squeal in anguish every time I stretched to tackle. But this wasn't my only problem. There was pain in my foot. I didn't know what it was, but the jagging, sharp pain in my heel got progressively worse every time I put my foot on the ground. It got to the point that I couldn't walk barefoot in the changing room and had to go on the toes of my left foot to avoid the excruciating impact of bone against the cold, hard floor. Limping on to the treatment table for the latest strappings and bandages of protection BEFORE the game starts is never particularly encouraging in anyone's eyes. But that's the way it was; I'd do anything to keep playing.

The pain in my foot was becoming unbearable though and eventually I succumbed and had to confide in the club doctor (like the physio, another member of the infirm's secret society). An x-ray was organised to confirm the extent of any damage I'd caused by continuing to play. The diagnosis was a calcaneal heel spur – a repetitive strain injury whereby a build-up of calcium juts out from the bone, causing a tender, pointed edge to protrude beyond the surface, hence the pain. It is particularly common in ageing females; effectively I had the left heel of an old woman. There were two options – an operation to shave the spur from the bone, or an injection to alleviate the inflammation and tenderness to a level which was manageable. The surgical procedure wasn't going to happen as the club had long since stopped paying their medical insurance. This is always the first thing to suffer as clubs cut back and the physio's supply room becomes as bare as a jakey's cupboard the day before his Giro is due. Everything from energy drinks to bandages become unaffordable luxuries. My only hope was another cortisone jab that would keep me playing until the waiting list subsided long enough for me to have the op on the NHS.

The club doctor administered his very own form of Lanarkshire acupuncture, although the inaccuracy of the first effort ensured a second injection was necessary to quell the inflammation. The only reason I know the first one missed the spot was because, second time around, the doc wriggled the needle until he found the EXACT spot of intense pain and I've never experienced anything as excruciating as that metal needle touching my tender bone. A necessity to ensure the steroid itself hits the spot, I was told. By now though, he was going to need ladders and a needle 6ft-long to reach my heel as I hit the roof with pain.

After I recovered from the shock, the steroid started to work its magic and I was able to play on for a bit, but the heel spur was performing under duress. Had it been able to talk, it would've been screaming at me not to be stupid, that I was only masking the issue and likely to do further damage. But I was back playing and that was all that mattered. I soldiered through the next few months. Painkillers and artificial sole inserts, called orthotics, helped a little but I knew I had months to wait until I could come off the waiting list and prolong my time in the game. Those next six months were to change not only the course of my football career, but also my life as a whole as liquidation, takeovers and the inevitable collapse of my fragile left foot all took hold.

*

As you will have gathered by now, the world of a journeyman footballer is an insecure one. The contracts clubs hand out are, by necessity, short-term and loyalty and honour are rare commodities. It would be easy to become cynical seeing how the game, with all its machinations and manoeuvring, really works from the inside. But, however much we moaned (and footballers are among the biggest moaners you'll find anywhere) there's ample compensation in getting paid to play football. Paid to play football! Maybe not very much and maybe not at the most glamorous of levels, but you're still earning your living doing what millions only dream of and many would willingly swap their higher-paid, more secure careers with you in a heartbeat. And one of the biggest privileges is being able to appreciate the abilities of teammates and opponents as only someone who's played on the same park as them can.

I took a call from Steve Archibald out of the blue. As I said, when players leave football clubs rarely do they keep in contact with teammates although I had cause to speak to Steve on a couple of occasions after he left Hibs as I helped him out when he set up a small coaching school. He was by far the best player I ever played with, an incredibly talented guy. In truth I never really rated him when I watched him on TV and couldn't really see how he'd made it to Spurs and Barcelona, but that opinion soon changed when I trained alongside him. His technique and movement were magnificent, but I've never seen before or since any footballer with more self-belief allied to the iron will and selfishness that took him right to the top. He was a loner, but when he decided to drop the defences he was very good company.

Steve was now an agent working from Spain and had heard there were quite a few young players pushing their way into the Airdrie team as a result of the cutbacks and wanted to know if any of them were decent. What he was really doing was sounding out the situation at the club and seeing if it was a viable option to take over, but I had no idea this was the case at the time. I presumed he was hoping to cash in on some promising youngsters in need of an agent and gave my opinion on who might be able to play at the next level. With that, the niceties were over and it would be six months before I spoke to him again.

Meanwhile, rumours of administration and liquidation were rife and more and more bills went unpaid. There was no corralling of the support like at Hibs and Thistle; instead the apathy borne out of the club's nomadic existence meant that if it was going to be saved, it would have to be by another method of raising the hundreds of thousands it was going to take.

KPMG were appointed provisional liquidators in February 2000. This knight in shining armour is a company that wallows in the misery of others, racking up astronomical bills as companies are wound down and tea ladies are sacked to save 50 quid as the heart is ripped from communities. As a senior player and union representative I attended the first meeting with KPMG alongside the manager and board members. What we heard was much, much worse than we could've imagined. The club's debts had now spiralled beyond reasonable control and dwindling crowds meant they were highly unlikely to ever be back on an even keel. Airdrieonians was dying.

KPMG had been in talks with various parties about taking over the club as a going concern, but survival meant the most savage of cuts. We were assured by KPMG that if we could get some of the higher earners off the wage bill, as well as cutting back on staff at the stadium, they would be in a position to transfer ownership and Airdrie would still be a football club. A compromise was reached whereby everyone at the club, players and staff, would take a 50 per cent pay cut for a month to buy the time for KPMG to do the deal that would allow the club to survive. This would at least ensure there were no player redundancies and we could keep a team on the pitch. We were assured by the parasites preying on the carcass of the club – while earning an eye-watering hourly rate – that we would all receive every penny back we had sacrificed during the month from the new owners.

Scottish football wasn't exactly awash with cash at the time and most of us had families to look after and mortgages to pay. The average wage at the club at the time would have been around £400-£500 so it wasn't as if there were millions in the bank, although I'm sure most, like me, had some 'rainy day' money locked away in an offshore account in Sauchiehall Street just in case. As long as the rainy days never lasted as long as a typical British summer, most of us could survive the short term. Unfortunately one month became two and two became three as the heart continued to be ripped from the club.

On the pitch the team was also suffering with the

cutbacks taking their toll on young players and senior pros alike. As Rangers have found to their cost in recent years, level of performance and team spirit suffer to such an extent that survival becomes more important than playing well. It didn't help that many of the players felt that the board had completely mismanaged the club and now, in their time of need, directors were resigning left, right and centre. The picture painted at the time was that they were resigning for the good of the club and the situation, but we felt the majority were getting out in order to protect their own business interests and avoid any financial liabilities.

Whatever the reasons, the players were left to pick up the pieces on half wages. I was rarely more than 60-70 per cent fit but, given the situation at the club, I felt a responsibility as a senior player and a union representative to stay aboard the sinking ship and continue to put my legs through the wringer. I was playing through a mixture of painkillers and anti-inflammatories which meant that, even if my heel was getting any better and the swelling was ever coming down, I couldn't feel it. It was a recipe for disaster. And when it happened, not only did I feel it, I heard it.

St Mirren were visiting our horrendously named home ground and my football world was about to be turned upside down. The Saints centre-back chipped a ball in behind me for their centre forward to run onto and it was a race between the two of us to see would get on the end of it. The Saints striker that day was Mark Yardley and rarely did anyone have to go into overdrive when chasing big 'Yards'. Predictably, I got there first, but, when I made to turn, there was

120

an audible pop in the sole of my foot right at the point of my heel spur. A sickening, gentle pop. Something had gone. The cortisone steroid had weakened the area so much that the tendon holding the front and back of the sole of the foot, running across the arch, had detached from the bone. I was in trouble alright as my plantar fascia had ruptured and my foot was now hanging like a string vest from a clothes line. It was bad. I knew instantly it was bad, and that my whole future as a footballer was in jeopardy. I was already on a 50 per cent pay cut, no longer capable of playing and out of contract in five months' time.

As I mulled over my situation from the discomfort of a hospital bed I consoled myself with the fact I at least had the cushion of getting back the three months' pay I'd sacrificed at 50 per cent, when the club was back on its feet again, as KPMG had promised in that first meeting. At the very least, that would give me another couple of months' rainy day money: enough time to decide what I was going to do next. Three months turned into four and then into five as the club sunk deeper and deeper into oblivion and, with it, I was forced to consider my next step. I couldn't give up so I went to speak to our glorious administrators only to be told there was no money to pay for my operation. If I wanted to give myself a chance of continuing to be a footballer I had to find the money to go private NOW.

The notion that their employers couldn't afford medical insurance would be alien to many footballers, and not even those regarded as top stars. But, even if that was the case paying for their own operation wouldn't be a problem. I was never a high earner, though, and after 14 years as a professional footballer I was forced to seek help from the bank of Mum and Dad in order to prolong that for a few more seasons. My parents were a huge support to me throughout my career and we managed to get the operation booked and paid for it ourselves, another example of their care and generosity to me. I'm sure over the years my brother and sister would have got a wee bit of help with something they needed, but it was never advertised in our family. Money was rarely spoken about in our house. You worked hard, you earned your pay and you got on with it. But you helped those close to you when they needed it. Angela and John will have been given just as much as I was over the years, but you would never have known it. Humility never cost anything.

I had the operation to remove the heel spur and re-attach the plantar fascia tendon, but the worst thing was that I was going to be out for approximately nine months. This would take me to the end of the season, through the end of my contract, and beyond the following pre-season into the new calendar year. To say my future was uncertain was understating the blatantly obvious.

I took another call from Steve Archibald and this time his intentions were much clearer – he wanted to take over the club. Steve would never give anything away in our conversations, but I knew how he operated and suspected he wouldn't take the club on whilst there were huge debts and players' wages to be honoured.

KPMG were still making noises about potential buyers, but Steve's name was never one of those mentioned. I got the feeling they never trusted him, but it was KPMG that we players didn't trust. After initially being told that a four-week wage sacrifice would be enough leeway to secure a buyer, 18 weeks later liquidation was to be the course of action and the majority of the players lost their jobs. Contracts wouldn't be honoured and the only people who would be paid were KPMG, who by now had become a major creditor. It all left a bitter taste because 18 weeks back salary, paying for my own operation and the remaining four months of my contract meant I was owed the grand total of £14,111. It could've been 10p or a million pounds and it wouldn't have mattered; I would never see a penny of that cash and the battle for survival was about to start all over again.

Some of the players had been asking me what was going on. It was common knowledge now that the club was about to liquidate and Steve was to take over, having finally convinced the administrators of his credentials. The truth was that I knew very little about what was happening, but it seemed fairly obvious that the manager, senior players and highest earners would be first out of the door. It's always the way in those situations and I couldn't see this one being any different. Only the players seemed to believe that I would know who was staying and who was going. Steve and I never had that particular conversation, but some of the lads felt I was stabbing them in the back.

We sat around that morning waiting for the new owners to come in and tell us who'd be staying and

123

who'd be on the dole. The changing room was like a morgue. Players paced anxiously up and down, wondering if they were surplus to requirements. I was worried more than most because not only would I be unemployed, I was also injured and had no prospect of playing. With a new flat and mortgage to service, it would have made things very difficult. Those of us not pacing the floor sat, silent, awaiting our fate. We wanted to train, but weren't sure who was staying and who was going and no one wanted to leave that dressing room until their fate had been sealed.

Then the changing room door burst open.

'You better fuckin' give your man a call!' Gary Mackay's face was contorted as he shouted at me. He clearly felt I knew more than I was letting on and he'd obviously just been told by KPMG that Steve was taking over.

'We need to know what the fuck's going on. Who does he want for training?'

I genuinely had no idea which players would remain and who was being released and was as uncertain as anyone about my future. I could feel the spotlight turning on me and, at times like that in a dressing room, all that footballer mistrust and individual self-preservation is spilling over. I got up and could see every player asking me if they'd be okay with their stares.

'I'll call him.' I moved slowly out the dressing room door with expectant, anxious eyes drilling holes deeper into the back of my head.

'The gaffer has asked me to call you to find out

124

what's happening,' I said when Steve picked up. 'We need to know who you want to train and who you don't.'

Steve's reply was quick, assured and brutally frank, although I expected nothing else.

'The senior players are all gone.'

'Steve,' I said, 'It's not my place to go back in there and tell them. I've played with these guys for two years, they're my teammates.'

Not only did I have to protect myself from the baying crowd, I also couldn't go in there and tell a man of Kenny Black's stature that he'd been dumped on the scrapheap. It wasn't my job and, as far as I was concerned, 'all the senior players' included myself. So I went in and told my teammates the only lie I told during the whole sorry saga. I told everyone to train and that they would find out after training and over the next few days who was being released. We went ahead as 'normal'. That is, if normal is a flat, desolate session devoid of any great activity. How could it be anything else with the majority of players going through the emotional wringer and one or two deciding not to train at all?

Over the next few days the decisions were finally made and an assortment of Spanish journeymen and the odd hidden nugget were flown in by Steve to replace the last of the Beastie Boys in a cold, and by now, rather depressing corner of North Lanarkshire. The majority of players had been thrown on the scrapheap, other than a few young ones who could potentially make the club some money, plus myself. Steve sat me down a few days later and told me that his consortium would continue to pay me whilst I recovered from injury and then, when I was fit, a decision would be made about my future.

I wasn't stupid, I knew what that meant. As soon as I was fit again I'd be out the door, but I would do everything in my power to show that I had something to give and complement the newly-formed Spanish Armada. I don't know whether Steve felt a sense of loyalty to me due to the fact I was injured, or whether it was down to helping him with that coaching school but it definitely wasn't part of a pre-organised plan. Regardless, I couldn't be fussy at that point and, for once, I couldn't think of my teammates. I had a mortgage to pay and at least I had the security of my wages for the next four or five months.

Unfortunately, I knew that some of my pals in the team wouldn't see it like that. Clearly it looked like I'd been helping Steve with the takeover and had been given a contract as a 'reward' for my endeavours. The fact that it wasn't the case was almost irrelevant. I knew what it looked like and I knew that some of the lads would perceive it that way. Sandy Stewart and Gary Mackay in particular felt I'd betrayed them. To Sandy's credit he told me so face to face a few years later and it was clear from what he was saying that he was speaking for a few others as well. Gary Mackay never spoke to me for a few years and if we ever crossed paths, a very cold, tense atmosphere was inevitable. Several years later we were forced to work together in a professional capacity when I was assistant manager at Dundee and he was working as an agent, which would at least soften our relationship. I never had anything but respect for

Sandy, Gary or any of my other Airdrie teammates but I know for certain they lost theirs for me. A lot of water has passed under the bridge since then, but I believe to this day that they feel I shafted them and I'm not sure I'll ever be able to convince them that I knew a lot less about what was going on than they thought.

After a long-term injury you are never pain-free. Six months after the operation I was finally able to run again. You jog until the pain won't let you go any faster and then you maintain that pace. The next week you might reach half-pace and are able to maintain that for a while before succumbing and then the following week it's ramped up another notch before you are finally able to go (almost) flat out. The next stage is to re-start training when the pain from the injury is eventually at a manageable level. Struggling, hobbling and carrying your way through training, but NEVER pain-free.

I was on a non-contract basis while continuing to try and fight my way back to business. Pre-season came and went and I was no nearer showing that I could play again, never mind make a contribution to the team. The side Steve had established featured very good players like Jesús Sanjuán, Antonio Calderón and David Fernández, but there were others in the group who weren't up to the level for which they had been brought in. I wasn't able to contribute on the pitch but I made sure I had a presence off it. I never missed a game and I was always trying to integrate the Spanish players into the Scottish morals of team spirit and ethics. As such, I organised a few team nights out to bring everyone together. They were successful, but I was never really convinced the Spanish lads bought into our 'the team that drinks together wins together' attitude. The 'them-and-us' mentality within the dressing room wasn't poisonous or too detrimental, but cliques had started to form in place of togetherness.

Steve was continuing to honour his part of the deal by paying me out of his own pocket while I tried to get myself fit. Although it was out of necessity, with the club going bust owing me 14 grand, I still felt uneasy picking up my wage packet every Friday. It wasn't the way I was brought up, to take and not give and it went against a lot of my morals, but I had no option, I needed that money, and so, it was back to my lonely world of rehab to see if I could get back playing at that level.

Mentally draining and physically exhausting, there are days when dragging yourself from the treatment table is as much exercise as you feel like you can muster. What keeps you going is the knowledge that if you don't do the core fitness and base strengthening work, the day will never come when you're finally able to pull on the sharpened metal studs. Not for me the new-fangled moulded sole. Grass was made for studs, not for roller blades. Double sessions of fitness work are almost always the order of the day when you were injured. I had been through it all before with the knee injury at Hibs, but it didn't get any easier to cope with. The nearer it comes to being ready to play, the tougher the workouts are and none of it is ever pain-free.

128

The strain being put on my feet by my dodgy knee and my running style, adapted to alleviate stress on the ruptured tendon, meant I was starting to ache elsewhere. It's common for footballers who have had long-term injuries to experience a period where they get aches and muscle strains in different areas from their acute injury. Pain management means adjusting the body to take stress away from the injury, causing strain elsewhere. My knee was squealing again and my foot was in a lot of discomfort, but it WAS manageable with the help of the orthotics and a considerable bandage, but something still wasn't right. The bone on the inside of my foot was now aching just below the ankle. There was only one solution; I would have to call on Dr Hypodermic again.

The professional advice is to have no more than three steroid injections over the course of your life but having had one on my knee and three on my foot already, one more wasn't going to do me any harm. If it could settle the injury just enough to get me back playing, then it was worth the risk. The tendon on the inside settled down after that fifth injection and my rehab was almost complete. I was fit (well, patched up) and could now resume full training. After eight-and-a-half long months of toil, sweat, pain, receivership, administration, injections and turmoil, I could finally look forward to playing again and showing I was worth keeping. I knew I was up against it. Steve had never hinted at anything other than me being paid until I was fit again, but, even though my foot and knee were about as mobile as the leg on a solid oak chair, I hoped to convince him to give me a contract until the end of the season. That would give me a further six-month trial period to prove to people I was fit and then I could weigh up my options through the summer.

I know now that I was deluding myself. Although I was now training every day and looking like I was fitting in, I was carrying the foot rather than walking on it and each session was becoming more difficult to recover from. I'd have been better with an AA van sitting outside the house in the morning to jump start my legs and take me to training, rather than relying on my clapped out Astra.

When the day of my comeback finally arrived, the adrenalin that had been missing from my veins while I slogged my way through those gym sessions and strengthening exercises was back with a bang. I could hardly feel any pain in the foot, although my left medial ligament was refusing to succumb to the anaesthetic rush that was coursing through my body. Livingston at Glasgow Green was to be my AC Milan at the San Siro. Livi had a fairly strong reserve team at the time due to their SPL status and yet another dubious signing policy bankrolled by a millionaire that was to end in disaster. Will our clubs ever learn?

Anyway, it would be a decent test even though I was only to play a half, or an hour at the very most, on physio's orders. As the game kicked off I found myself charging about like an 18-year-old again, only my touch was all over the place. I kept over-running the ball, my passing wasn't exactly spot-on and my timing was slightly out, but some would say they never noticed the difference. Physically I felt fine and my fitness was good – a testament to the

130

tough strength and conditioning work I'd done to prepare myself for this moment. The foot was holding up, just.

Donald Mackay, the new Airdrie manager, asked me at half-time how I was feeling.

'Great,' I said.

'Another 15 minutes then?'

'Aye, definitely.'

After 60 minutes I gave the thumbs up. The 70, 80 and 90 minute marks all passed and I'd played through my first full game in nine months. I was elated, ecstatic and it COULD have been the San Siro for all I cared. I was back, fit (ish) again and I'd showed I could still play a bit. I was looking forward to a day off to recover and then training on the Thursday. Maybe now that I was fit again I could even sneak a place on the bench on Saturday for the first-team. I was racing ahead of myself of course, but, as far as I could see, I was no longer tarnished goods. Unfortunately I was to be brought back down to earth just three days later, with an earth-shattering thud.

My legs had stiffened up sufficiently enough by Thursday's training session to let me know that I wasn't quite ready yet for the first-team, but as I tiptoed gingerly through that practice match, I still harboured unrealistic ambitions of making it. Friday's session came and went and, as I picked up my wages before leaving the ground, I was called back to see Donald. Maybe they're going to draft me into the squad after all, I thought. When I walked into his office, Steve was standing beside him and I could sense from the atmosphere that what I was about to be told wasn't good. Well, not for me anyway. I've subsequently learned to put on that face myself when releasing young players. The sycophantic, well-meaning game face that portrays your sadness and regret at the situation. It's a front of course, put on to try and soften the blow for the recipient until the time comes to do it all again and this time it was my turn.

'We're going to have to let you go David. We think now that you're fit again it would be better for you if you moved on and got yourself a new start.' Another classic managerial deflection. Make it sound like you're doing the player a favour. The reality was they didn't want to give me a contract in case I broke down again.

'Cunts!' I screamed at them; inside my head at least. In truth, I couldn't have any arguments. They had fulfilled their side of the bargain by paying me for five months while I was getting myself back to fitness, so my actual parting note was a lot less confrontational.

'Fair enough.'

132

The Cortisone Years 2000-2004

Clydebank
Stranraer
Albion Rovers

I left Hibs for football reasons. Like any other player I wanted to play at the highest level I could. I knew early on that I would never get beyond the Scottish Premier League, but I also wanted to prove that I could play a bit and to do that I needed to be a regular starter, a first pick. Joining one of the favourites for promotion offered the chance of doing that AND getting the possibility, in a season's time, to be doing it at the level I was leaving now. Had I known what I know now, I may never have left.

When you start going down the levels, you rarely come back up. The only chance you have is when the lower-league team you join is able to bounce straight back up and you get carried along with them. That was the plan at Thistle, but financial mismanagement and, on the back of that, a weakened squad that was never going to be good enough put paid to that.

What I'm about to say is hardly the most romantic view ever taken of football, but the higher a point you start off at, the longer it will take you to fall to the bottom. Despite their years of experience in the game, football people can be as susceptible to supposed pedigree as fans. Faced with choosing between two trialists of obviously similar ability, most will opt for the one with Manchester City and not Motherwell on their CV. If you're freed by City after your apprenticeship you'll probably find another English club at a good level willing to take a chance on you based on where you came from. The same in another two years' time when you end up at a Scottish top level side. Even after a few seasons of failing to establish yourself in the first-team you might even eke out another three or four years at various full-time clubs before you find yourself at your level – playing part-time in the Scottish League One alongside the former Motherwell trainee that's been there since he was 19. That guy may have turned down Man City when you signed for them because he thought he'd more chance of breaking through at Motherwell. He did, but he still wasn't good enough and he found his level a lot quicker than you did as a result.

A two-year contract was on the table at Hibs and after that I might theoretically have got another four years as a full-timer outwith the top flight before finding myself in the situation I was in after leaving Airdrie – listening out for a phone that wasn't ringing and staring the dole queue in the face. My foot and knee were no longer likely to stand up to full-time training. The continual pounding and pressure of daily sessions would put too much strain on an already creaking body. Football is a torrid, unforgiving environment and God forbid you should have a long-term injury because everyone– coaches, managers, players and staff – talks. It was fairly obvious that word had been put out that I was struggling to get back to full-time fitness and it began to dawn

136

on me that not only would part-time football be the only way I could keep playing, I'd also need to start WORKING for a living.

Samantha and I had begun talking about starting a family. We were still living in separate flats in Dennistoun, but it was time for us to sell up and move in together. In truth, we should have made that step a few years earlier, but my selfishness and dedication to my football career put paid to that. The idea that having children would in some way be negative to my career has to be one of the most perverse trains of thought anyone has ever had, but it was really as much about me being able to swagger around the east end of Glasgow, every inch the footballer. Well, I wouldn't have looked the part, popping down to William Hills to put a coupon on with the pen and betting slips in one hand and baby's bottle in the other, would I? I'd reached another crossroads and not only needed to prove myself as a footballer all over again, but also find a way of supporting the family I was planning. First of all, I had to find someone, somewhere, who would put a piece of paper in front of me to sign.

Shettleston Job Centre wasn't exactly the place I had in mind, but sign on their particular dotted line I did. For about six weeks, I was unemployed.

During that time I trained with Clydebank in order to keep myself fit (relatively, as always). If I could get a game in the Second Division then I could at least show that I was still capable of performing at some level. Clydebank led a horrible, nomadic existence at the time with no ground and no facilities to speak of and they were soon to go out of existence as

137

a knock-on effect of the Airdrie situation. They were living out of the back of manager Tony Fitzpatrick's car, with his boot resembling a kit room, but managed to maintain a professionalism that belied the club's circumstances.

They were unable to offer contracts at the time due to their situation, but were to make one small gesture that I'll be eternally grateful for. At the end of my three weeks there and having played one game (a 4-2 defeat at Arbroath) I was handed an envelope by Tony with £300 in it. John Viola, a football agent, was indirectly involved in the consortium running what was left of the club and he gave me three weeks expenses out of his own pocket. Someone giving something without wanting anything back was a rarity indeed in football. That one gesture let me know that not everyone in the game was heartless, there were one or two good guys out there after all. They weren't ALL in it for themselves. It wasn't a huge amount, but it was something I've never forgotten and it certainly supplemented my £51.50 per week buroo money. But back to the Job Centre it was.

Job Centres are depressing, desolate places that breed humiliation and contempt. I was a footballer and I shouldn't even have been there. I'd earned all that money and the millionaire lifestyle of a superstar, hadn't I? The 14 grand I was down after the Airdrie debacle really grated now but, having paid enough taxes over the years, the Job Centre was an option I had to embrace. Despite the fact I was never a big name, I used to enjoy the odd person knowing who

I was as I walked about the east end of Glasgow and nudging their companion to say 'he's a footballer, you know'. Most people in the Job Centre wouldn't have known me from Adam, but that didn't make me feel any less humiliated as I walked in the door. I automatically bowed my head and kept it low in the hope even fewer people would be able to recognise me. I always bought a newspaper before I went in as that would give me another excuse to keep my head down away from the inevitable glare. In reality I probably didn't need to as half the people in there were so off their faces they wouldn't have known if David Beckham, never mind David Farrell, had walked in.

The fortnightly ritual, 10:20am, on a Wednesday. Walking past security, flashing your card and then heading over, head bowed, to your waiting area. At this point I would only have to go through it for the next six weeks, but when I left Dundee later in my coaching career, I'd have to endure months of it. That's the thing about these places, no one goes in there with their head held high and no one EVER comes out feeling better about themselves.

There's a pretence around the system that they're there to help you find work, but in my experience, and that of thousands and thousands of others, it's not the case. More often than not, the whole intention of the staff and the regulations they follow is to get you back off the unemployment list, somehow, anyhow. It doesn't matter to them if they find you a job, or that you get so fed up with the trudgery and desolation of the place that you decide to never go back. Either way, UB40 are no longer singing about you and you can be ticked off their pathetic list. They have targets like everyone else and their target is to remove the statistic that you have become so that you are no longer registered 'unemployed'. They'll arrange meetings for you with trainers and job 'coaches' that have no relation to your circumstances. Most of them couldn't coach a shite out of an arse. Should you miss a meeting or decide not to bother, that's it, money cut or worse still, suspended. They also make the forms and process so difficult to fill in the first place that it becomes a chore to even be registered in the world of the unemployed. DLA, JSA, SSP, a world of worthless acronyms. Well how about this one – GTF.

So here I was, waiting my turn, and I'd take out my phone to avoid eye contact with anyone else. I didn't want to look at anyone, bump into anyone or speak to anyone. Then, in their infinite wisdom, the Job Centre banned mobile phones due to the sensitivity of details they held and a desire to stop people unscrupulously gleaning information. I found this out when the security guy came over and told me I wasn't allowed to use my phone on the premises.

'I'm not using it. I'm looking at it,' was my reply.

'Well you can't look at it in here.'

'I'm looking at job sites for vacancies, trying to find myself work.'

'Not in here you're not.'

I almost fell off my chair. The irony in that statement was obviously lost on this particular Einstein of the security world.

'BUT IT'S A FUCKIN' JOB CENTRE!!!!'

140

With that, I was asked to put the phone away or leave the premises.

Now my pride really wanted me to lob this particular Nokia at his head and walk out the door, but that would mean the system had won as I wouldn't be able to sign on and I'd be off the list and my £51.50 per week would be down the pan. Because that's part of what these places are all about, driving you into the gutter and getting you off that politically driven points scorer, the unemployment figure.

I was occasionally lucky that there were two people who worked in there that I knew and, if I managed to get one of them I'd be away from their desk fairly quickly, sparing me the inane monotony. If I didn't, I'd be praying to at least get a man in the hope he might recognise me (a little sexist probably, but it's a fact that only 10-15 per cent of season ticket holders are women). This time I thought I'd struck the jackpot as I sat down opposite a nice gentleman and handed over my book, filled in with the names and contacts of people I'd called looking for a club, agents, managers, players etc. Showing that you actually are looking for work is a condition of being unemployed and if your paperwork isn't filled in properly you're in trouble. I used to fill mine in on the Tuesday night, making it up as I went along. I'd phoned this coaching school and that community programme. It was a load of bollocks because, at that point, all I wanted to do was get back playing, but by Wednesday morning it looked the part. Looking at my book you'd have thought I'd more contacts than an internet dating site. I would show them I could play the numbers game too.

141

'Oh, you're a footballer,' the guy said. 'I don't really follow football.'

Just my fucking luck! The words that would guarantee the going through of every single question and the ticking of every box, prolonging my agony and humiliation.

'Have you done any work, paid, or unpaid in the last fortnight?'

'Have you been actively seeking employment?'

'Have you filled in your job enquiry sheet?'

'Have you lost the will to live yet?'

Hope was on the horizon, however. I finally had a club interested in me and the most sought after signature in Shettleston Job Centre was heading for the southernmost club in Scotland. I was about to become a part-time footballer.

Any illusions that I was a big-name capture were to be shattered on a cold night in front of a post-war record low attendance of around 120 fans. I hadn't gone to Stranraer for the glamour and the town most definitely hadn't turned out en masse to welcome their new signing, but it was great to be back playing. My debut was against, of all teams, Clydebank and it ended in a desperate 0-0 stalemate. I signed until the end of the season to prove to the club I was fit enough to earn a longer contract, but I also hoped I could prove myself worthy of a full-time contract somewhere else. I was deluding myself again as neither my foot nor my knee would stand up to full-time training and matches at that level. Football does that to you though, it toys with your rational thought and tries to convince you that you can still do it, but you always know in your head when you are kidding not only yourself, but also your employers.

I was fit enough to be a part-time player for the next three-and-a-half years and, while I had no choice but to accept it AND find a proper job, it wasn't easy to take that on board. I'd been a full-time footballer for 14 years and although I'd started on the coaching ladder at Largs a few years earlier in preparation for this moment, it was still a shock to the system. I played out the season through gritted teeth as the muscles had started to creak with the strain of being back playing, but only training for three hours a week over two evenings enabled me to perform to a reasonable standard. I was playing sweeper behind two lumbering centre-backs and I was able to use my football brain to compensate for the lack of athleticism caused by the odd running style, orthotics, cycling shorts and strappings.

I managed to find myself a job too, with a training company who worked with teenagers who had either dropped out of school or had little or no job prospects. We worked out of a community centre in Moodiesburn and I devised a curriculum designed to engage with them through sport and general literacy. The owner of the company, Mark Shanks, was an ex-professional footballer who only ever employed fellow ex-pros, mainly because he reckoned that, with all the shit thrown at them throughout their careers, they had a work ethic and resilience that would stand them in good stead for this particular line of work.

Some of these kids were no shrinking violets, but, to me, it was no worse than dealing with a dressing room full of egotistical players.

Importantly for me, Shanksy's understanding of the demands of part-time football meant I could leave work early when required. I had to adjust quickly to doing a day's work before heading to training on a Tuesday and Thursday, but luckily for me the physical exertion was minimal – just as well given my body's record for reliability. I played out the rest of the season and was offered a one-year contract. Stranraer were a well-run club and paid fairly well for the part-time level. I was given £200 per week plus £50 expenses to cover the costs of getting to and from training. My two jobs took me back up to what I was earning at Airdrie and getting me back on an even keel again. Even more importantly, I would be number two to manager Billy McLaren, which would give me some experience of coaching and managing at first-team level. I had been coach of the Under-13s at Airdrie, but this would be my first taste of being on the REAL 'dark side'.

The final game of that season was to be, as far as I know, my only experience of another kind of footballing dark side. Almost every player I knew enjoyed a bet. It was part of the culture, but it was never seen as wrongdoing, unless, of course, you were betting against your own team. It wasn't as complicated back then: there was no first throw-in betting, five-minute markets, both teams to score or bookings (I'd have made myself a few quid on that one) and personal accounts were the bastion of the addict; those who couldn't go half an hour without a punt on who had the hairiest legs.

Players these days have to be aware of the public scrutiny and the pitfalls of the press and social media, but I used to casually make my way down Duke Street to the bookies on a Saturday morning wearing my Hibs club suit. I'd shove my coupons on without batting an eyelid, or raising an eyebrow of suspicion from anyone else, before heading through to Edinburgh for the match. If it was an away game we'd get on the bus and head to our chosen hotel for our lunchtime pre-match meal and then, as long as there was a bookies nearby, spend a half-hour getting our coupons on. This was a ritual played out by players, managers and coaches throughout my career and I'm sure many fans over the years have been greeted by the sight of 12 hairy-arsed players, all in their club tracksuits, scrambling over bookies pens and coupons in their Turf Accountant of choice. It was one of the things you had to organise on the bus down – who could remember the bookies nearest to the hotel in Forfar or Berwick.

It's become very easy to bet on anything in football these days and the internet has made it such big business that corruption could inevitably become a factor. Many players have slipped into the murky world of gambling addiction. While I've always enjoyed a punt it was never a problem for me, but I can see how it could be very easy for lower league players' heads to be turned by the promise of riches for making a specific event happen in a game, either on the back of a gambling debt or just pure and simple greed.

Go to any Under-20's development match up and down the UK and you will see guys on phones and tablets instantly relaying information back about a specific match to betting syndicates or the bookies themselves. Players who don't earn a lot of money could quite easily become targets for those looking to influence the outcome of matches. Thankfully, it would be very rare for a match in Scotland to have been corrupted, but I played in one 14 years ago, although I had no idea about it until after the match.

We arrived at Shielfield Park in Berwick, hardly a hotbed of football and certainly not where you would expect to hear of a game that was apparently 'a bit dodgy', ready to go. Although we were still playing for our £50 win bonus it was really a meaningless match as Berwick were three points ahead of us in third place and, barring the proverbial cricket score, we were destined to finish fourth. We started the game particularly well and went ahead after just three minutes and doubled our lead not long after. Half-time came and went and we played the game out comfortably for a 2-0 win. It was a very hot, May day, the pitch was rock hard and we had played very well considering it was a classic end-of-season affair.

Shielfield Park was unusual in that there was no particular Players' Lounge to go to after the game but the Social Club is adjacent to the stadium so we were given permission to go in for an after-match beer with the opposition players and fans alike. That post-match situation is a generally relaxed affair. Players know each other very well and, contrary to popular belief, animosity rarely, if ever, carries

146

over. Even mixing with the opposition fans is a very civil affair and this occasion was no different. The usual small talk ensued, but there was one Berwick supporter who was insistent in revealing something telling.

'There was only ever going to be one winner there today,' he said.

I assumed he meant that, since the league positions had effectively been confirmed the week before, Berwick had nothing to play for, so I agreed that it was always difficult to get motivated at this time of the season.

'Half the town was on you to win today and the other half don't gamble,' he was only too happy to tell me. 'One of the local bookies has taken a hell of a beating.'

I spoke to one of their players and he confirmed that one or two of the team had been in on the action with the punters. I have to say that it didn't feel like the game was in any way 'bent'. The tackles were flying in and arguments raged over petty throw-ins as they would normally. I just thought we played well and never had one second of suspicion until the Berwick fan decided to spill the beans.

I believe that football in Scotland will be amongst the most honest of games worldwide, but players will be tempted from time to time. I had a bet on the team I was playing for at what I perceived to be good odds on many occasions, but I was never one for backing anything in big sums and not once did I bet AGAINST my team. I couldn't do it, but I've no doubt that many players over the years did. That

147

doesn't necessarily mean that they would have actually attempted to throw a match and those Berwick players would probably only have stuck a couple of quid on the opposition to hedge against the likelihood of losing their win bonus. Because lower league players in Scotland are among the most honest and dedicated you'll find anywhere.

Part-time players get a raw deal, because the commitment they show to play while holding down a full-time job in many aspects puts some full-time footballers to shame.

Many supporters of so-called smaller clubs will be put out by the disparaging reference that clubs in financial difficulty may have to go part-time, as if that's some sort of slur or put down. The truth is that many of our part-time teams live within their means and are run on a much more business-like basis than many of the full-time clubs they're supposed to aspire to be like.

Of course, as you move down the leagues, the standard of play AND player deteriorates, but the effort and desire to play football doesn't diminish. I suppose I could've made things easier for myself had I not signed for Stranraer, with the logistics involved in getting to and from matches, but they had recognised that getting players from their own catchment area would be impossible, which meant we were able to train in Glasgow. We were always very well looked after, leaving Glasgow at 10am on a match day and stopping at the local hotel for a pre-match meal, a luxury rarely afforded to any part-time outfit. A final bonus was that I was able to work with Billy McLaren, a veteran of many clubs and the only manager I've ever come across who was able to skip seamlessly from amiable to indomitable in a matter of seconds. He was a highly intelligent man and so well-mannered that to meet him in the street you would never believe there were many times in my capacity as player/assistant manager when I had to convince him not to rip the head off one of his own players. But he was a wonderful, old school, football man. A part-time football man in the loosest possible sense.

Billy had a very good full-time job working in the tax office and his senior position allowed him the flexibility to fulfil his managerial duties. It always amazes me when you hear of the part-time player who has a 'sympathetic' boss or the manager who is 'very understanding' when the player needs time off. I'm convinced a lot of it is anticipation of the time when the press are pushing for a romantic story ahead of a big club v wee club cup game. 'Aye, ma gaffer at Chunkerton, Phillips and Webb solicitors has given me the afternoon off so I've got time to get to Pittodrie.' We all love a bit of free publicity and our egos polished now and again. Football does irrational things to people and even the most hardened supervisor on the shop floor seems to fold in the face of a possible giant killing.

Billy's football philosophy was simple. If you had more possession of the ball than your opponents, you should win. Everything was about passing, one-touch, two-touch, keeping the ball. In that first year it worked for the most part as we finished respect-

149

ably mid table. But it also meant I wasn't getting a lot of coaching experience. Training was all about the small-sided games, passing drills, and possession football. We very rarely did any tactical work, which meant my title as player/assistant manager was a tenuous one to say the least. I wanted to coach, to set the team up and work on strengths and weaknesses, set plays, anything that would make me feel a little more worthwhile in the position. The time constraints at a part-time club – only having a couple of 90-minute sessions a week – meant very little other than fitness and basic technique work could be squeezed in. The Monday/Tuesday fitness session I was to encounter at Albion Rovers was as tough as any session I ever did at a full-time club, although my weakening limbs would be spared for now due to Billy's 'total football' philosophy. There is a certain level of fitness your body can reach and a part-time player having played 12 games in a row will be no less match fit than his full-time opponent.

The gap between the average full-time teams and the better part-time teams is nowhere near as vast as pundits and experts would have you believe, but the mentality to approach the first session of the week having been down a hole or humping bricks on a building site all day is a strength of character unrivalled in football. Dragging a well-worn body around laps of a public park after a 12-hour shift is far from the idealistic vision of a professional footballer, but if I wanted to keep playing this was now my reality. I'd accepted that I was no longer full-time and had to start carving out a career path outside the game as the opportunities I craved in coaching and management were all too fragile and infrequent.

Towards the end of that second season at Stranraer, I was to get the literal kick in the balls that would change my life, although, on this occasion, it would be in a positive way.

By now, the training company I worked for had merged with Cumbernauld College. I was employed to deliver the course I helped devise to young trainees at football clubs throughout Scotland. This was perfect for me as it meant I had the stability of a 9-5 job within the public sector while continuing to network around the game. I could effectively tout myself to the clubs and make them aware that I wanted to be a coach, should any opportunity at their club present itself. I was playing part-time, teaching full-time, and hawking myself like a Bombay money lender to anyone who'd listen. It was shameless, but allowed me to keep playing whilst holding down a decent job.

The teaching part was a natural progression for me. I'd never been quiet and had always tried to be a positive influence on young players, but this was different. As soon as I became employed by the college, I had to get qualified. Going back to school wasn't easy. Dissertations, exams and portfolios and all in a timescale that would have pushed Stephen Hawking to the limit. Days would consist of work from 9-5, training from 6.30-8.30 and then home to study until midnight. If there was a midweek game it would be after midnight before I got home, but at least I could do some studying on the team bus. The glamorous life of the Scottish footballer, and yet I still loved it. You can't beat pulling on that jersey at three o'clock on a Saturday, no matter the division nor the circumstances.

Samantha would have had as many children as I agreed to, but my selfishness to preserve a fading football career and a perceived image to protect meant I had resisted, foolishly, until the end of the 2001/02 season.

We played against Stenhousemuir at Stair Park and I went in for a trademark, straight leg tackle with their midfielder. I was used to players pulling out when I went in like that and I rarely came off second best, but this young lad clearly didn't respect the reputation I had carved out. I would have been the same myself, making sure I left my mark on a senior pro just so he knew who I was. The crunch of the challenge was magnificent and I admired the lad for smashing into me. His boot continued its path and, like an Exocet mapping its devastation, his studs smashed into my unprotected family allowance. Remember, this was 13 years ago and gentle, forgiving blade soles were only for the superstars. The rest of us still wore boots with six, razor-sharp metal studs and, I can assure you, four of my opponents' cleats were now nestling in my undercarriage.

As was my way, I got up, although very, very gingerly. I didn't want to show him he'd hurt me but on this occasion my only option was to sit straight back down again as the pain was excruciating. I had a quick look down. There was no blood so I knew that, if the pain settled a bit, I'd be able to carry on. I hobbled through to the end of the game and limped, like John Wayne with rickets, into the shower. By now my right testicle had swollen to twice the size of the left

152

one and the wee man was looking more dishevelled than a Gorbals street fighter on a Saturday night. My first pee after the game had the cloudy red appearance of a sweet and sour sauce. I never told anyone I was peeing blood, hoping it would resolve itself.

By Monday the swelling had settled but the bleeding, although much fainter, continued. I called one of my old club doctors, to see if he could squeeze me in for a quick appointment. This doc had administered a few of my stitches and been present through a couple of my concussions so he knew me well and that I wouldn't be calling him if I thought it was something trivial. He'd once given me two stitches at the side of the pitch without the aid of an anaesthetic – like forcing a knitting needle through a leather football was how I would have described it – so it's fair to say we were old adversaries. After a quick one-two of the crown jewels, a straightforward 'bruised urethra' was diagnosed. As long as I didn't do anything silly I'd probably, unbelievably, be fit for the following Saturday. As it was, the scare had convinced me that if I wasn't careful, I'd wait too long before trying for a family. Even though I was only playing part-time, I was happy with my lot. Samantha and I both had good jobs. I was about to sign another one-year contract with Stranraer and we were going to start a family. Nothing could possibly go wrong, could it?

I managed to get through my 17th pre-season without spending my £1500 signing on fee and, just before our first friendly, we found out Samantha was pregnant. I approached that first game as I had every

153

other, although the fact it was on astroturf at Glasgow Green filled me with a little trepidation. With my record for injuries and a foot that was as fragile as the family china at a Greek wedding, artificial surfaces were the last thing I needed to start the season on. My professional pride wouldn't allow me to sit it out but, after just 20 minutes, I was regretting my bravado. That niggling, stabbing pain on the inside of my ankle, where two of my five injections had taken place, was back. I knew it had gone again, but I played on until half-time and then broke the news to Billy that I'd have to come off. I knew the big man well and I could tell that he felt something wasn't quite right. I hoped, as I always did, that it might settle down but you know, you always know, when you aren't right and so I built up the courage to go and see the specialist. He took a look at my foot and had a prod about at the inside of my ankle, then flicked through my medical history, which contained details of the knee and foot operations.

'You're going to have to quit playing,' he said. 'If it's painful now and collapsing on you it's only going to get worse.'

Being honest, I only heard the first part of the sentence. The rest of it I'm only guessing at as I stopped listening at 'quit'.

'Isn't there a chance, something we can try? How about an injection?'

'But you've already had two.'

I'd been economical with the truth when asked about my history with cortisone. The trap was laid and I was ready to play my trump card.

154

'But isn't it recommended that you have no more than three?'

'It's recommended that you don't have any!'

After some gentle persuasion and cajoling I had an appointment for the following Thursday. During that time I sensed a different attitude towards me from the people at the club. Billy was looking uneasy and, although no one said it to me, the sudden, frosty reception I was receiving when I arrived at Stair Park on the Saturday to cheer the boys on told me everything I needed to know. They thought I'd stitched them up. I wasn't stupid and knew that they felt I'd signed a new contract and taken a signing-on fee knowing I was injured. I wasn't that type and there had been many times during the previous season when I shouldn't have played at all because of hamstring, groin and calf strains and dead legs but put myself through the pain barrier for the club. I saw what they thought that of me as a slight on my character.

At that point all manner of things were running through my head. If I couldn't shake it off this time and really did have to quit, maybe I should just tear up the contract and give them their money back. That would be the honourable thing to do, but it would also seem like an admission of guilt and I wasn't having that. There was only one thing for it, I HAD to get fit, and so I returned to Ross Hall for my dose of football adrenalin. I knew right away that the doctor had missed the spot. The excruciating, tell-tale, white-knuckle pain hadn't been there. It was still painful and uncomfortable, but the jaw-dropping stab when the needle hits was missing.

All the while the whispering campaign reached fever pitch and I could feel the hostility from the hierarchy at the club. Handshakes were now limp and grudging and, even though I knew I hadn't diddled them, I was feeling the heat. Three or four weeks passed and I still couldn't get fit. I wasn't quitting yet though and the fact the club were now questioning my integrity meant I had to convince the specialist to give me one last hit. I pleaded for another 30ml of cortisone and, whilst he wasn't keen, I'm sure the £105 consultation cost must have swayed him just a little.

I sat back and waited for the horrendous, excruciating pain of needle against joint. The wiggling and manoeuvring of the one-and-a-half inch hypodermic tip, was as always, uncomfortable. And then he was on it. It must be similar to that of a junkie waiting for the heroin to hit his vein, when he knows the pain he's putting himself through isn't right and is doing serious, long-term harm, but he knows the short-term gain that needle brings makes it all worthwhile. Injection number seven was in and this time I knew he hadn't missed. At that point I wasn't even worried how short the short-term would be because I knew I'd be lucky to get another two seasons out of it and still had my full-time job to fall back on but I was driven by a warped sense of pride. I had to prove to them I hadn't signed a contract under false pretences. I would play again, even if it meant the long-term consequences could be drastic to say the least. After 10 days, I could feel the cortisone coating the inflammation and suppressing it to such an extent that I trained flat out for the first time in three months. Two or three sessions later and I was ready to join our campaign.

In truth, I was probably rushed back a little quicker than I'd have liked, but we had a small squad and it was all hands on deck. Part of me also suspected that they'd rush me back in the perverted hope that I'd break down again proving them right, but that may just have been my cynical football mind at work. We played Motherwell, an established SPL side in the Scottish Cup, and we handled them well for an hour before going down 4-0 as their quality told. I was up against James McFadden and more than held my own for that first 60 minutes before he started to drift into areas that were difficult for me to follow to. Maybe if I'd have had younger legs and a more agile body I'd have been able to go after him and kept us in it for longer, but it was encouraging for me and for the team that we had matched them for long periods.

I was at least back playing although my hamstrings and groins were by now straining at every sinew to accommodate the weakness in my foot and knee. Samantha had given birth to our son, Lewis, and we were ready to sell our flats and move in together. I loved Dennistoun, but by now it'd become a little rundown and plagued by trouble and violence, so we felt it was better to take our family out of that environment and move to a quieter area. I made the right choices when I lived there but felt if I could give Lewis and my step-son Harris a nicer environment to grow up in they might not need to make as many choices and would enjoy better opportunities.

We were playing some nice football, or at least as nice as the Second Division could be. With a dozen games to go we were only six points off a promotion spot. However, such were the vagaries of the league that particular year we were also only 10 points from the relegation zone. The whole league was squeezed together like an accordion on the 12th of July. We kept playing our way, but results were sucking us closer to the danger-zone and I could see the players were starting to get nervy, a common trait among teams drifting towards doom.

I wished we would change our style and be more direct, play in the opposition's half and keep the ball as far away from our goal as possible, but we persisted with the passing style that Billy was rightly proud of. We went into the final game needing to win at home to Airdrie (of all clubs) to have a chance of staying up. We lost 2-1 and, with that, our fate was sealed. Incredibly for a team in a 10-team league, we had gone down with 44 points. We had finished 9th and yet had only finished 11 points behind the promoted team in second position. But none of it mattered, we were down. I was sitting beside Billy on the bus back from Stranraer and he said to me in his own, polite, immaculately spoken way 'I never saw that coming Faz, did you?'

I did what every good player/coach does in that situation and I lied through my teeth. 'Nope, I thought we were going the other way.'

I was a fraud. I'd felt for months that our style of play meant we were too fragile defensively and too vulnerable to teams who played a more physical game. I knew, being the man he was, Billy wouldn't have changed, but I should at least have tried. Now, I was bottling it again simply because it would cause a lot less confrontation on the bus on the way home. I never shirked any kind of challenge in my whole career and had stood up to the strongest of managers but, for once, I let it go.

Billy quit immediately after that final game and a little part of me selfishly resented that, because had he done so with four or five games remaining, I might've been given the opportunity to go in as caretaker and turn things round. Maybe keep the team up and retain the manager's job for the following season. With the service he'd given the club, Billy had earned the right to hang on and try to keep his team from the drop, yet here I was falling into the old selfish footballer trap.

I hoped I might be considered for the manager's position, but also knew that with my contract up it would be easier for the club to release a 33-year-old crock and free up the wages. The only thing that disappointed me was that no one ever called to say that, not only was I being freed, but that I'd no chance of getting the job. It was a great wee club that had until now prided themselves on doing things the right way, only this time they hadn't. But that was professional football and I still hadn't had enough of it yet.

My playing record shows I was, for varying lengths of time, at seven different clubs. Hardly Ryan Giggs stuff, but nothing compared to some. The list of former clubs on some players' Wikipedia page reads like an A-Z of footballing backwaters: three games here, four games there, a substitute appearance somewhere else.

Journeyman as I was, I had the luxury of the odd two-year contract during my career and spent at least a season with every one of my clubs, with the exception of my Clydebank cameo. I never had to endure the merry-go-round of trials, loans and short-term emergency cover deals that more and more players do as they try desperately to get some traction in the game.

One of my responsibilities at Dundee was to sift through the weekly mountain of letters, CVs and DVDs of players looking for a trial. It quickly became a case of disregarding most as unheard of, or not having played at a good enough level. One or two would catch the eye and a follow-up call would be made to player or agent. DVDs were the most difficult to assess as it quickly became apparent that even I could've trawled my Mum's loft, cut a few Betamax tapes of my days on Sportscene and mashed up a DVD that made me look like Platini.

Clubs regularly circulate details of 'Players available for transfer' or 'Players available for loan'. Quite often you can easily substitute the word 'Player' for 'Problem'. Some players on loan are prospects for the future, but, more often than not, they'll have been deemed surplus to requirements. There's a perception that loan players don't care as much about their new club as they do their parent club, but I've never known a player to try less or be less committed because he's on loan, especially as he knows he's likely to be given the heave shortly and has to earn himself a new contract somewhere.

After leaving my sixth club and, given my personal circumstances and deteriorating physical condition, you might have thought it was time to call it quits. My glory days, such as they were, were well gone and I'd suffered blow after blow in the game. I had a stable, reasonably well-paid job that offered the possibility of progression and left my nights and weekends free for my young family. While part-time wages weren't substantial they helped with the new mortgage, but continuing to push my body beyond breaking point also increased the chance of more serious injury that would stop me earning for my new family of four altogether. And all for the chance to, maybe, if my legs held together, match players who wouldn't have been able to lay a glove on me a few years earlier.

It was obviously a no-brainer.

I wanted to be a manager, I REALLY wanted to be a manager, but the most difficult part is getting someone to take the chance on you. There were an awful lot of coaches and managers out there who would take any opportunity given to them and who were more qualified than me. I had to keep in the football environment if I was to have any hope of that happening so, for the first time since I was 18, I was about to go on trial again.

The Sun had organised a trial game for out-of-contract players. The managers or coaches in attendance were easily outnumbered by representatives of the newspaper who were looking to show how much they care and how much good they do for the game. I strolled through the game and was able to prove to myself, if no one else, that I could still play a bit. I went home and sat back, waiting for the phone to ring. Eventually, after two weeks, Peter Hetherston, the Albion Rovers manager, called. The club had narrowly missed out on promotion the season before, meaning they remained in the Third Division. It had taken me 18 years to fall from the top division in England to the bottom one in Scotland (see?) and I couldn't have been happier.

Albion Rovers were a well-run wee club. The ground was ramshackle and decaying and the dressing rooms were past their best, but they certainly looked after the players and never spent anything above what they could afford. My teammates included a few other veterans playing out the end of their long careers and young, ambitious guys, a lot of whom had stepped up from the junior ranks. They saw establishing themselves at the Rovers as the first step towards making it. That first session was the last of the pre-season and I felt it was important to make my mark and show them I still had the legs to make a contribution. Bad idea.

Throughout my career I'd been a 'middle of the pack' runner, sitting in behind and hanging on to the coat-tails of the leaders. I was never athletic enough to lead out and the 'Kenyans and Ethiopians' of the squad would always leave me in their wake as they kicked for home during a track session. This time though I led them out on an 800m run to shouts of 'Go on Faz, string them out' from Peter. I lasted barely halfway before tumbling backwards as my legs felt like someone had exchanged my boots for concrete blocks. I could hardly raise a gallop. In the past I'd have started to go back and then hung on to the leading six or seven, but this time I limped home with the stragglers and the goalies. Injuries meant my body was starting to resemble that of a backstreet beggar, but when fit (relatively, remember) I could still keep up with the best of them.

This was the first REAL sign that my legs were going. I'd have to manage my training schedule and probably step out when it came to the tough early week sessions in order to preserve my energy for games. It was a balancing act though, because not doing enough would leave me lacking in sharpness.

We trained on a Monday at Dunbeath Park, known locally as Dogshit Park, and on a Thursday at Cliftonhill. After every Thursday session we'd be treated to a plate of hot soup and bread and I'd receive my small brown envelope with my £150 (less tax) in it. Always cash, always on time and never short. It was a brilliant wee ritual and the spirit it harnessed would have put some full-time clubs to shame.

We started the season fairly well, but I could see we had no chance of sustaining it and going up. The young lads were full of energy and commitment, but they just weren't good enough and, as soon as we got one or two injuries, we'd struggle. I was getting frustrated in training and, rather than being a good influence to the young lads, I was being narky and argumentative, shouting instead of directing and looking after myself instead of leading. It was another sign that my time was coming to an end.

On the pitch was the easy part. The standard in the Third Division was such that I could've played some of those early season games with a suit and brothel creepers on and still got away with it, even half-fit and with legs that were by now taking four days to recover. In a home game against Arbroath I was straining to catch a tricky winger and launched into a slide tackle from too far, opening up my old medial ligament injury. I soldiered on through the next couple of games but I was nowhere near right. I couldn't turn to my right without carrying my knee round in an arc and had the mobility of a seven-berth caravan. Players who honestly couldn't lace my boots were leaving me for dead.

It came to the point during one of those games in the aftermath of the injury that I resolved to tell Peter I needed to rest the knee. I would do it as soon as I got off the park but first there was another striker who had given me the slip to chase. It was approaching the cold, harsh, winter months and I tore my calf muscle.

Being a footballer recovering from injury means spending a lot of time in a lonely, desolate place. The weeks following a serious injury are the most difficult. You can't run yet, but you need to do anything possible to keep up your aerobic fitness levels. Day after day in the gym – exercise bikes, weights, rowing machines and swimming all serve as your companion in the 'non-weight bearing' part of getting fit. It can be tortuous work, broken only by the early morning ritual of being on the end of the physio room banter. Injured players are always in first in the morning, preparing and getting a dose of shortwave treatment or some manipulation on the affected area. The physio's room is the social hub of the club every morning as the players come in for their strappings, bandages and mollycoddle rubs. You feel part of it for half an hour as you join in with the banter, the stories and the spirit and then they all leave for training and you go back to your very own solitary confinement. Because at that moment, you are a nothing, of no consequence until you are fit again. You have no value to the club while sitting on that table, alone with your thoughts. The gaffer will occasionally pop in and ask how you're doing, but he's only paying lip service. I've done it myself as an assistant. Go in and cajole the injured lads, give them a wee boost and let them know the gaffer is thinking about them then head straight to the his office decrying the waste of money lying on the treatment table for half of his contract.

It's bad enough at a full-time club with that daily break to look forward to and where you might even have the best medical support science can muster on hand – oxygen chambers, ultrasound machines, ice baths, warm baths and physiotherapists with more qualifications than an online university. But this was Albion Rovers. We didn't have a physio room for starters and the physio himself was only there one night a week, so if you wanted to get fit again, you were on your own. The away dressing room (the smallest in the country) doubled as our medical centre with its 25-year-old treatment bed slapped bang in the middle. This was going to be a slog alright and I wasn't looking forward to it.

Two weeks into my latest rehab we lost Peter Hetherston after an off-the-cuff remark about Scotland's first female match official was manufactured into controversy and he resigned. My former Hibs teammate Kevin 'Crunchie' McAllister, who was also now plying his trade with Rovers, took over and I had missed my chance to be caretaker manager again. I expected him to make me his assistant, but the club decided they wanted the experience of Frank Connor to help him as it was his first job in management.

165

Having been bypassed for both the manager's position and that of assistant, I set about pounding the track at Cliftonhill through the cold, winter months to at least get myself back playing again. I'd been getting treatment once a week and trying to run three times a week for six weeks, but I just couldn't shake off the calf strain. Every time I stepped up the pace to the nearest I got to sprinting I could feel the calf tightening. Mentally, it was destroying me.

I put my bedraggled training kit on again to exit the Cliftonhill tunnel for yet another session of lone drudgery and stepped on to the frozen gravel track. As the club couldn't afford to put a floodlight on, I was negotiating the rutted, rock hard surface alone in the dark. It was minus three degrees and, even though I was trotting out lap after mind-numbing lap, I could barely get up enough speed to warm my fingers let alone my ageing muscles. My foot was aching on the hard ground, my knee was throbbing and my calf was as tight as it could possibly be.

I slowed down to rest and gingerly walked back to my starting position, cold breath blowing steam on the way out and tightening my chest on the way back in. I was just about to start another lap when I stopped, took one last deep recovery breath and asked myself 'what the fuck are you doing here?'. It was pitch black and freezing. I wasn't even a 'might have been' anymore. I was a has-been and I'd had enough. The training, the running, the cold, the dark, the washing my own training kit, the rushing away from work to make games, the endless fucking backstabbing and the injuries. I made my mind up there and then I was quitting at the end of the season.

There were no tears and no dramas. In actual fact, I was relieved. Relieved that I didn't have to pretend anymore that I was fit and that I was still enjoying my football. Relieved that my family would see more of me and that results would no longer determine my mood for a particular weekend and relieved that I would no longer have to put my body through the pain and agony of constant fights back to fitness. It was over and, at that moment on the cold, dark track at Cliftonhill, I was at peace with myself. I still had a few months left on my contract and I would honour that out of respect for Kevin.

I waited until training on Thursday before I went to see him because I wanted to give myself a day or two to make sure I wasn't just coming to a decision because I felt sorry for myself, wallowing in my own self-pity and just looking for someone to boost my ill-informed football ego by telling me I still had something to offer. But at that particular juncture Sir Alex Ferguson couldn't have convinced me I would still be a player beyond that season. I informed Kevin of my decision and told him I would continue to work as hard as I could to get fit and be a good influence on everyone around the club. I also told him I would walk away now and make way for some youngsters if he felt that was the best thing for the club. We agreed to play things by ear and, after I eventually got myself fit again in February, I played another half a dozen or so games before the end of the season.

I helped Kevin from the sidelines as best I could and tried to ensure the players bought into his way of playing. I'd help to keep the quality and standard of training up and wouldn't allow the young players to clique together and slag off anything he was doing. He'd shown me great loyalty since I told him I was quitting, the least I could do was try to get him the job on a long-term basis.

On the last day of the season, he told me I would be starting at Stranraer (again, of all places) and that I would be captain. I was ecstatic and ran about that pitch like I was 16 again. Even though we lost 4-0 and Stranraer won the league that day, I played well. It showed me that, when I was fit, I could still play a bit. I had approaches from a few of the bigger Junior clubs to play another season, and take a hefty signing-on fee into the bargain, but I couldn't do it. It was unlikely my body would have stood up to another full season and, after my experience at Stranraer, I wouldn't let myself be sullied by accusations that I was a washed-up old pro who'd only signed for a few grand and a polishing of his ego. And I didn't fancy an eighth injection to prove myself.

In the dressing room after the game, wee Crunchie announced to the rest of the squad that it was my last game and that I would be quitting. I was a professional footballer no more. The reception I received from the players was incredible and only enhanced the feeling that I had made the right decision. It was emotional knowing it was over, but even then I couldn't shed a tear in front of the players because the mask, which had protected my hard-man image over 18, battle-scarred years, couldn't slip even now. I sat there, perversely, rather contented. I'd done my bit and lived my own football dream. The only question was, what the fuck was I going to do now?

Money, Money, Money
2004-2008

Gretna
Dundee

As a profession, football has statistically one of the highest rates of both divorce and depression, post-career. Keep that in mind the next time you think your striker doesn't care when he misses a chance or the defender makes so much of a hash of a pass back that it ends up in his own net. The main reason for that statistical spike is that you can rarely replace that fix from your playing days.

Managers and coaches will do almost anything to remain in the game and avoid a lonely, football-free existence because those deemed surplus to requirements are very quickly ostracised in this harsh environment. It's easier to get another job in football while you're in employment because, believe me, when you are out of it, the phone stops ringing. No agents punting trialists, no managers enquiring about your star midfielder and no fans stopping in the street telling you how great a job you're doing or how well you're playing. It is why, more and more often, managers with decent track records will take a job in the lower divisions to feed their addiction. Nothing compares to it. It's almost masochistic because you never get the same feeling back you had as a player, and it's far more stressful than playing ever was. But you always strive for it, hoping the next job you have is your key to the big time. But, of course, life rarely works out like that.

The few weeks that followed my last game were strange. I never felt the depression that was supposed to overcome you when you stopped playing. I was working full-time through the summer so a lot of the time that could've been spent wallowing in self-pity was taken up by work commitments but I felt relief, most of all. Relief that I no longer had to put my body through 14-hour days just to make ends meet and furnish my under-inflated ego. Relief that there would be no more injections, no more muscle strains and no more arduous, demeaning fitness tests to prove I could last another pain-filled 90 minutes in the bottom tier of the Scottish Football League.

Then, when the realisation that I could no longer call myself a footballer kicked in, I realised the huge void was there after all. I wanted back in. Players always talk about missing the dressing room and the camaraderie, the banter and the spirit, but what they really miss is the involvement at all levels. The ability to watch games for free, to turn up at grounds and have a complimentary ticket waiting for you. The handshakes as you take your seat in the stand and bump into all the old faces. The falseness of the greeting as you embrace the coach who freed you 10 years previously and pretend it's all water under the bridge while despising him as much as you did then. The training and the addictive buzz you get from being fit and the recognition from fans that point and nudge as you take your seat. That's what you really miss because, when you leave the game, it all stops.

While a sprightly 26-year-old at Hibs, I had started to prepare myself for a life beyond football by going on the first of many coach education licence courses at the Inverclyde National Sports Training Centre in Largs because I always wanted to become a manager. The stress and the power of the position, the leadership, the shaping of a team, they all appealed to me. Making the tough decisions and being the bad guy wasn't something I had any issues with. After making a career out of being a bastard on the pitch, I was sure it couldn't be that difficult to be one off it. I'd certainly worked under enough managers and been in enough dressing room situations that I knew how not to do things. I was ready for the next step, but first I had to get qualified.

It took me seven years and eight qualifications before I could say that I was a UEFA 'A' Licence Coach. I was still playing at Stranraer at the time, but I'd long seen the way football was going and knew it wouldn't be possible to get a coaching job or a managerial position without having the qualifications. Joining the so-called 'Largs Mafia' was the only way to go. Largs has earned an international reputation for delivering exceptional coaching courses, but also one as being home to an illuminati of football coaches who run the game in this country like a secret society. There is an important distinction between the administrative side of the SFA and its coaching structure. The blazers have no real input in the grassroots and

173

only make the decisions from boardrooms and ballot boxes. The 'Largs Mafia' however very often dictates which coaches will work where, and which managers will be in with a chance of being the next Jose Mourinho or Sir Alex Ferguson.

I was well aware that I didn't have a big enough name to get a job through reputation alone so I'd no choice but to immerse myself in the clique. Many coaches get jobs in this country (or at least their first opportunity) through recommendations from other coaches within the game and, in particular, from those within the Largs corridors of power. A nudge here or a wink there often results in an appointment. I always found it difficult to suck up to the right people. It wasn't really my style and, during the long, arduous days at Inverclyde, it would sicken me to see players fawning at the feet of the experienced coaches they hoped might give them a favourable mark or the inevitable nudge in the right direction.

The courses themselves are intense and involve coaching from 9am before moving on to lectures, fitness programmes, pre-season preparation, technological analysis and business studies. By 9pm you feel so overloaded with information that the first, relaxing pint of the evening goes straight to your head. Within minutes, the sauce bottles and pepper pots are mapping out a 4-4-2 on the table, two cocktail sticks jammed into a beer mat for goals and your pint glass playing in goal as you work out how to combat the overlapping vinegar bottle. I sailed through the 'B' Licence, managed to pass the 'A' Introductory course with flying colours and was ready to tackle the full 9-day UEFA 'A' Licence assessment the following year.

Inverclyde brings together the landed gentry of Scottish football, the international players and top stars with the not-so-glamorous unknowns. Not only would I be locking horns with them in a football sense, I'd also have to eat, sleep and drink with them too. Socially I wouldn't have a problem because the east end in me would come out after a few drinks and I felt confident that my coaching ability was up there with them as well. I believed I could do it, but I also knew I was under pressure from the start.

It was widely known that, regardless of the standard of their coaching, the big names would generally gain the qualification unless they suffered an absolute catastrophe. As the names of my group of 12 were read out I knew instantly I was up against it – Packie Bonner, Craig Levein, Jimmy Nicholl, Owen Coyle, Terry Butcher, John Robertson, Chris McCart, Des McKeown, me, two unknown youth club coaches, and an American we ended up nicknaming 'My Bad' for obvious reasons.

I knew the pass rate wouldn't be as high as 10 out of 12 so that meant that, with the six internationals probably passing and big Chris having been on the fringes of the Scotland team there were only a couple of places left. There was the possibility that one of the unknowns might get a certificate if they were to perform exceptionally well and make the process look like less of a stitch-up. By my powers of deduction, it came down to a straight fight between me and Des.

The first couple of days on the course are spent observing the staff coaches run through the themes and explaining how you are expected to perform and behave as a coach. Team shapes, formations, twin strikers, defending as a back four, overcoming offside, penetration, the counter attack, countering the counter attack. The information was mind blowing and the intensity of sessions was physically and mentally draining. I was in my element, enjoying the learning process and trying to prove that I could be a coach. Even though I felt the pressure of being assessed and scrutinised at every turn, I was performing well. The staff coaches at Largs were great football men putting on fantastic sessions and imparting the knowledge they had amassed over decades in the game.

Each night we'd head down to the local hostelry to join the other group and discuss how the day had gone and how we would go about delivering the next day's theme. I'd be sitting with Terry Butcher and Packie Bonner, who could boast nearly 200 caps between them, deciding whether HP or Heinz should play up front and manoeuvring condiments to see where the striker should be in relation to the mustard. It was bizarre and brilliant.

The programme began in earnest on the third day and I was immediately aware that my hunch about pass rates and probabilities wasn't too far off the mark. I led my first session around the theme of twin-striker play. I was comfortable and competent in front of the group and delivered a good programme, or so I thought. Jimmy Bone, my staff coach and mentor, delivered feedback that amounted to a below-par performance. I'm honest enough to admit when I haven't done well and, whilst I may have lacked a little experience, I felt the appraisal was unfair.

As I suspected, myself and others on the course were being set up for a fall. I continued to try and work on my perceived failings for the rest of the nine days. Reverting to my default setting of insecure footballer, I would ask my peers how they felt I was doing and hope for a boost to help me approach my final assessment with confidence. They were telling me all the right things, that I was doing well and that I should have no problem passing from what they had seen. If I'd been true to myself I would have confronted Jimmy and told him that I felt that some people had passed before they even turned up at Largs and others never had a chance due to the need to preserve the pass/fail ratio while protecting big names. But I also felt that confrontation would probably result in me never achieving the required 'A' Licence. Indeed, some of what I've already said in this book may well rule me out from ever coaching in Scotland again, such is the influence of the illuminati in the closed shop that is Scottish football's hierarchy.

I went through with what I felt was a fairly decent assessment on the final day but, by now, I knew it would have to be exceptional. I waited three weeks for my outcome, going through the same kind of torture I had waiting on school exam results. When word finally came through in the form of a beautiful, headed note from Technical Director Craig Brown, I only took in the first five words: 'We regret to inform you...' All seven big-name players who were on that course with me performed well and none of them deserved to fail, but I also believe that I had done as well as most of them and better than one or two. I was angry and my dreams of applying for managerial positions in the lower leagues and building a reputation for myself were lying in tatters. Yet again, the game had kicked me in the balls.

I vowed there and then not to give up and immediately reapplied for the course the following year. I couldn't let it beat me. I had to show resilience and go back down there and pass second time around. I'd get £300 from the Players Union Education Fund to re-sit the course but I'd have to shell out the remaining £900 myself. I played out that final season at Stranraer with the same clear career path that many ageing, decrepit pros have in their head – get a coaching or managerial role somewhere and prove yourself before making it big. The reality, of course, was that the country was littered with experienced, out-of-work coaches, many of them far more qualified than I was.

I took a lot of sessions at Stranraer when Billy was away watching prospective opponents that season and arrived at Largs just as ready as the previous year but more determined than ever. We went through the same gruelling programme as before – 12-hour days on the training pitch intermittently broken up by seminars on psychology, lectures on fitness and conditioning and all manner of video analysis. This time round I was in slightly less heady company. Mercifully, 'My Bad' had decided that one year of starting a practice game with 12 men and coaching an underlap instead of an overlap was enough for any man and he'd gone back to 'soccer', never to return.

In truth, I didn't do as well as the previous year and the doubts crept in again, gnawing away at me and I knew that if I failed this time there was no going back. My assessment came and went and as I paced the hall floor at home waiting for the A4 envelope to

178

come through, my future as a coach hung in the balance. It finally dropped through the door and I ripped the envelope open then slowly revealed the letter's contents, a line at a time.

The name.

The address.

Dear Sir,

We are pleased to inform you...

And that was it, I'd done it.

I could have saved myself the drama if I'd noticed the letter was stuck to the back of a shiny, white certificate signed and dated by Craig Brown. I still have that certificate on my wall at home and every three years I have to attend 15 hours of refresher courses in order to re-validate my licence. It may not mean as much to some in the game as it does to me, and certainly there were some who were given it, rather than having to earn it, but the important thing for me was that it represented opportunity. After slogging my way through an 18-year playing career, I was ready for life on the other side of the white line.

As I said before, the fact Alex MacDonald and Alex Miller had played under the same manager as each other for most of their careers was something I found difficult to get my head around. I would wonder whose style was closest to Jock Wallace's and which Alex had spent years thinking 'I'm going to do things completely differently when I'm gaffer' at training each day.

Another harsh lesson that playing and coaching styles can be miles apart came when I joined Albion Rovers. I knew Peter Hetherston well and knew he hated running as a player, so I knew his training would be all about ball work and technical drills. How wrong I was. I'd forgotten 'Silky' had spent his later years at Airdrie and had clearly been converted to the cause of running until you dropped. This wasn't a welcome realisation for a 34-year-old whose body seemingly grew more brittle by the day.

My coaching philosophy was heavily influenced by my playing experiences, both good and bad, and all those 'shape' sessions at Hibs were to become a big part of it. My approach, and therefore that of most of the teams I coached, was based around being compact, difficult to beat, playing high up the pitch and playing with two strikers. Times have changed in just a few short years, with more flexibility in your system being essential for success these days, but some elements of coaching haven't.

Even the best coaches in the world can't make a silk purse out of a sow's ear and players need to possess natural ability for them to work with. In my opinion, coaches make teams better but rarely can they have such an impact on a player that they can make them better than nature intended. The difference they might make is to help someone become a better player by coaching them within a team structure that allows them to take up the correct position or make the right decision. This automatically makes the player better in terms of overall performance, even though their technical ability isn't improved.

It's in the interests of coaches for the opposite

180

to be believed, but the range of potential technical improvement is actually fairly narrow, especially by the time players reach first-team level. For me, one of the greatest coaching myths surrounds the supposed need for players to be two-footed. Someone who's good with his right but awful with his left will be lucky if his weaker foot improves by 10 per cent, no matter how hard he works on it... meaning it will still be shite. Whereas if his right foot is pretty good and it improves by two per cent it can become very good. In my eyes, it's better to work on the good foot and make it slightly better than to work on the weak one for a fairly meagre return. That theory goes against a lot of the accepted approach to coaching and, while it's undoubtedly influenced by my own experiences of working with what I had to make up for technical deficiencies, it's something I genuinely believe.

My first appointment after retiring was unlikely to ever allow me to turn coaching orthodoxy on its head but it did allow me to get that vital first foot on the ladder and meant my name was in a small way linked to one of the strangest chapters in the annals of Scottish football.

Bankrolled by the eccentric Brooks Mileson, Gretna had grand ideas and deep pockets despite hailing from a town with a population of 2,700, only 10 per cent of whom followed their local team. They were climbing the divisions and were intent on taking on the big boys. To do this, they needed a first-rate youth initiative and had recently appointed my ex-Hibs team-mate Danny Lennon to head it. They were setting up a satellite youth centre at Glasgow Green to try and cherry pick some of the best local talent and wanted me to help them with my contacts in the east end. We eventually took over two local boys' club sides to fill our under-14 and under-15 squads and used the trial process to put together the under-17s. When the money starts flowing, the system is abused and established boys' clubs and ailing community programmes are pillaged in the name of progress.

These sugar daddies are inappropriately named because what they end up doing to many of these clubs is far from sweet. These guys aren't billionaires, they're not Roman Abramovich or the Mansours or Sheikh Ali Akhbar al I've got More Money Than Sense. These are usually self-made and often well-meaning but they know nothing about running a small football club and do the one thing they shouldn't – they start throwing money at it and get in far too deep before they realise just how unsustainable things are.

Gretna was a prime example. A club in the lower divisions of Scottish football were paying players four-figure weekly salaries and setting up extravagant youth policies in Glasgow, all on crowds of 300-400. It would have taken Abramovich to sustain that type of model.

Being based in Glasgow meant I was rather detached from the club, but every time I visited the stadium I struggled to see how it could last. But I was in the game and that was the most important thing for me. I could support my family with my full-time job at the college and the part-time position at Gretna kept me coaching while I waited for that elusive phone call. I gained two years of experience and got an education into running a youth programme and co-ordinating

182

coaches, but it wasn't a particularly difficult task. If any problems did crop up, the extra budget was always found to pay for it but I would only spend what was necessary to keep us competing and my £75 per week for two nights' training and a Sunday match was hardly going to break the bank of Gretna.

I attach no blame whatsoever to the players, but there were a lot of hangers-on, who jumped on the great Gretna gravy train and were making a lot of money through Brooks' kindness and foolishness. People in the background, in positions of no importance or worth, were being paid very well indeed for hanging on to the coat-tail of a fantasy that ended up going horribly wrong. Some of them should hang their heads in shame now at the way they exploited the situation whilst knowing they were already being overpaid.

My time in the romance capital of the UK came to an end before things reached their inevitable conclusion. Gretna continued on their merry, irresponsible way, making it into the SPL, the Scottish Cup Final, and European football. Brooks was continuing to prop up the club through this meteoric rise through all four divisions in five years but the cracks had already started to appear. Impending rumours of Brooks' ill-health, had coincided with a downturn in the club's fortunes and after a struggle in the top division, the plug was pulled.

I had plotted a north-easterly course and left for pastures new two years before Gretna's eventual demise. I sincerely believed this might be my big break but it turned out to be another harsh lesson in the realities of football finances.

✳

The first thing any management team do when they arrive at a football club is analyse the strengths and weaknesses of the squad they've inherited. While Alex Rae and I knew we had a difficult task on our hands at Dundee before we even took over, the more we scratched beneath the surface, the starker the outlook became.

Alex's playing career had taken him to Falkirk, Millwall, Sunderland, Wolverhampton Wanderers and Rangers since our days growing up in Dennistoun, but we had remained close friends throughout the years. He called me in May 2006 to say he'd been sounded out about the possibility of taking over at Dundee as player/manager and asked whether I would be interested in becoming his assistant. On the face of it, this was a good opportunity. The club had recently been regularly finishing mid-table in the SPL and reaching the latter stages of cups. The potential of a good home support was clearly there and the ambition of the new board meant a return to the SPL was the ultimate, achievable aim, but there were many downsides that would make the job a difficult one.

The club had been ravaged by administration after racking up debts of around £20 million and the ongoing repayment obligations meant finances were constrained. The situation was compounded by the number of overpaid players who'd been kept on in an attempt to return to the top league at the first time of asking. A target that was disastrously missed when the club finished in their lowest ever position of seventh in the First Division the previous season.

This ailing Dundee club had just about limped its way off life support but remained in need of some serious emergency surgery. However, nothing about the challenge fazed me at this point. From the moment I received that phone call from Alex, I'd made up my mind. I was back in the game and back where I belonged, among football people. Back among the mistrust and dishonesty. Back where the agents tried to shaft you and offer you players they know aren't good enough or are injured, as long as it makes them a buck. Back where other managers will talk to your players behind your back and then pretend it never happened when they sign them.

And yet, I couldn't say no. This was my chance to prove I had what it took to be a coach. If Alex and I could be successful, we could make our mark in the game and I could forget about the fact that I'd thrown away a steady, comfortable job which could have become a career. This was the chance I was waiting for and I wasn't going to give it up. I had served my penance.

The previous summer Samantha and I had sat in the back garden, watching Lewis kicking the ball around and decided to have another baby. She had a good job managing a city-centre restaurant and I had my steady job at the college as well as my wee part-time number at Gretna.

Hannah was born in March and, at that point, we were comfortable enough with what we had. We had always lived within modest means, as most footballers do, but at that point I had stability. Samantha stopped working at the end of her pregnancy. I didn't want her to work anymore, I wanted her to be the full-time mother she had craved to be through all my years of selfishness. It became my driving force and motivation for the next 10 years and my excuse for leaving behind the stability of a teaching job to get into full-time coaching. Possibly the most precarious occupation in the country, and certainly that in the football world, but here I was, ready to risk it all.

My justification would be that this was our big chance; the full-time job. This would be the first step on the ladder to glory. We'd do well at Dundee and then move on to the SPL before being elevated to the Championship in England. From there, a mid-table consolidation and a recommendation from Sir Alex, the most senior member of the 'Largs Mafia', would get us in the door of the Premiership and access to Sky's millions. Big time here I come.

It was all so simple. My plan to provide for my family and make sure Samantha never worked again would be complete. First step, though, was convincing her that chucking my stable job and good pension scheme at the college was the right thing to do. She never once put any barriers in the way of my football decisions and she wasn't going to start now. She knew it had always been my dream to coach and manage. Dundee wasn't too far away so I would be home almost every night. As long as I was there for the kids, she'd have no problem with it. It was all a big front from me anyway because, if she had put up resistance, I'd have found a way to convince her. Nothing and no one would stop me as I was back in selfish mode, considering nothing but what I wanted. Back in the game. A two-year contract worth £25,000

186

in the first year and £30,000 in the second was to be my reward. Samantha and I wouldn't have much to spare, but we had enough to keep us above the breadline and that was enough for us.

The squad was on its knees and the playing budget was to be slashed from £1 million to £480,000, with many of the bigger name players released. Other full-time budgets in the league at the time would have ranged from around £300,000 to about £1.2 million at Gretna, so I would estimate ours was around the seventh highest. We didn't have time to dwell on our difficulties, however. We had to get a team on the pitch that could be competitive on a shoestring.

We knew promotion would be almost impossible that first year, but the important thing for us was to show that we could build and coach a team, organise them and make them competitive and fit. We knew that's what it would take to prove to the board we were worthy of a bigger budget to make a push for promotion in the second season, but our first task was an assessment of our human resources. I made my way over to Alex's cinema room for three nights on the trot (we could've gone to mine but the 24-inch portable in the spare room would have made for less comfortable viewing) and watched hours and hours of DVD footage from every home game the previous season. It was a stark reality check and this was us watching the team where the majority of the big hitters and the better players were about to leave!

All of a sudden the stable environment of the college, tutoring from 9-4, travelling just eight miles from home to work and then the odd training session at night, seemed like a much more desirable option.

I'd given up stability and security for this, but, as far I was concerned, it was worth the gamble. The team was disjointed and spread out all over the pitch like a Subbuteo team in the hands of an octopus, and they made life far from difficult for anyone who visited Dens. In fact, other teams looked like they were enjoying the big, lush, bowling green pitch more than the Dees were, and and demonstrated this by regularly passing the ball around them at will. The team were playing too deep and were so far apart and strung out, the back four were virtually playing at Tannadice while the strikers were in Lochee and the big pitch wasn't helping that.

We knew that the lack of quality we would have in the team due to the budget constraints (anyone we signed had to be on between £300-£500 per week) meant we had to be fit, organised and disciplined, but if our opponents were similarly prepared we needed some other way of giving ourselves an edge. We couldn't go toe-to-toe with the teams of a higher standard, so we had to make sure we were solid and compact and never allowed them to play. I remembered a ploy used by Graeme Souness at Rangers in a European tie against one of the best passing teams in Europe, Dynamo Kiev, when he shortened and narrowed the pitch. So that's what we did. We took eight yards off the length and six yards off the width but, not only that, we made sure everyone knew about it. We were trying to give our side both a physical and mental edge by getting into the heads of the other managers and players, hoping they would change their normal preparation and the way they played, thereby playing into our hands.

We gathered up all manner of waifs and strays from Scottish football – free transfers, trialists and troublemakers – all on an average of £400 per week. We added to the mix one or two of the younger players and some of the lads we inherited on the payroll. The board were about to allow Gavin Swankie to go back to Arbroath for a nominal fee because they were so desperate for cash, but we persuaded them to turn it down. Similarly, the best player we had was Kevin MacDonald. Kevin is now a million-pound player in England, but at the time he was on the verge of moving to Celtic for £75,000. We somehow convinced the board to resist and then had to convince the players to stay.

Come the start of the season we had managed to bolster team spirit. We were fit, organised and ready. As we watched the opposition managers pace their way across the pitch at Dens to see just how much we had lopped off it, there was an optimism all of a sudden that we could turn things round and take the club from the football doldrums back to football respectability.

We lost the first four games.

It may surprise you to know that, at every club I played for, one of the first things spoken about was the fans. 'What are they like here?' is always one of the first things asked upon arriving in the dressing room and the answer from your new teammates is always the same – 'murder'. No matter the club and no matter whether it averages a couple of hundred or

50,000 spectators, fans don't change the world over. When things are going well and you are winning, they're a little more tolerant of mistakes, but when things aren't going well, ALL fans turn. There are very few exceptions to that rule. We all like to think that we're better and more supportive than Celtic, or Rangers, or Stranraer, or Peterhead, or whoever your rival is, but the reality is we're all the same.

Dundee was no different but their recent history meant there was a particular frustration that heaped pressure on anyone who took the job. In just a few seasons they'd gone from being a top-six SPL side, competing in Europe and reaching cup finals and semi-finals to administration, relegation and despair. Throughout this the fans had remained terrifically loyal and had played a major role in saving the club but many seemed unable to grasp where it now stood in the pecking order – seventh in the First Division and unable to compete with part-time teams for wages on occasion.

The prawn sandwich brigade at Dundee were particularly vocal in their discontent and had more influence behind the scenes proceedings than any club I've ever known. The hospitality suites at any club are a hotbed of gossip as their inhabitants have the ears of chief executives and directors. It's a form of bribery, but clubs can ill-afford to upset these investors so a word in the right ear usually goes a long way. So along with the REAL fans screaming abuse at the chairmen up and down the country, and the investors making sure their wishes are adhered to with the odd threat of pulling out of their £20,000 executive box, you can see why managers are reluc-

190

tant to fawn their way around the lounges at the end of the game. There's no doubt in my mind that the corporate ranks played a major role in bringing Alex and I's time at Dens to an end.

Out of two cups and sitting second-bottom of the league, all our plans and ambitions lay in tatters within weeks of arriving at Dens. Dundee had a reputation as a sacking club and we were feeling the pressure, more pressure than I'd ever known in all my years in the game. When you're playing, you're engrossed in your own world, making sure you are in the team and looking after number one. I could always trust myself, but could I trust 22 players to turn it around, remembering some of them weren't that good? The pressure to succeed wasn't just about me now, it was about Samantha, Lewis, Hannah and Harris. I'd chucked a steady job, a comfortable position in the public sector, for this. And here I was staring the sack in the face again. It was the first time in my adult life I'd felt real insecurity.

My responsibilities and the family values my parents had instilled in me made me feel guilty for being so selfish and trying to make something of myself in the coaching world. The insecurity of not quite belonging in the Premier League as a footballer was nothing compared to this. The board said nothing and, while they weren't putting us under any direct pressure, we could feel it all the same. It comes from within, people looking and dissecting your every decision, judging every team selection and wondering whether they had made the right decision by appointing you. Directors rarely tell you this to your face, but you hear it from elsewhere – from secretaries, kit men and others who'll tell you questions are starting to be asked. Make no mistake about it, if it hurts and it matters to you as a person, then the pressure can become overwhelming. It hadn't got to that stage, but we needed a win.

We worked harder on the training ground with extra sessions on shape and the pressing game the pitch demanded, and the players embraced it. And then it happened. We steamrolled Clyde at home and it felt like a dumbbell was being lifted from my chest even though we weren't stupid enough to suddenly believe the squad we had was going to be good enough to sustain any kind of promotion challenge. The season was about consolidation and progression, about showing everyone that these two rookies had what it takes to put a team together. We were brought back down to earth the following week with a home defeat to Livingston and had the daunting task of a long away trip to title favourites Gretna the following week.

Anything less than three points would leave us with one win from the opening seven games and we knew that game could well define our time at Dundee. There are times as a coach when training and preparation goes well and you just get a feeling that something good is going to happen. It's something that's impossible to explain. There's no real reason for it and you haven't been doing things differently, but the sense of 'clicking' is there all the same. We travelled down to Gretna, more confident and positive than we really had a right to be given our indifferent start to the season and found ourselves 4-0 up before half-time. The travelling support was in raptures. The fans at Dundee always travelled in

192

good numbers and they were rewarded with free-flowing, fast, aggressive football as we went forward and a defence that was compact, tough to break down and organised.

We had to be careful after the game with the press, because an over-reaction could bring unrealistic ambitions and put us under more pressure to achieve more quickly than the team was capable of doing. It's a question that's often asked by fans, 'if they can play like that once, why can't they do it every time?' The answer is simple – THEY'RE NOT GOOD ENOUGH!

The ability to perform consistently is how you judge a player, not on one-off displays when all manner of factors could've gone in their favour. It's what makes good players better ones and what makes better players top ones. Players almost always find their level. It's why some players can score goals in the lower league but can't when they move up a division. The pace of the game is different. Sometimes it's slower, which means players who can't handle having too much possession struggle when they suddenly see more of the ball. Sometimes it's faster, which means they can't think quickly enough to be able to retain possession. If we built unrealistic expectations amongst the fans and press we'd be out on our arse in no time. Football management is about self-preservation a lot of the time. Set the bar low, consolidate and achieve a higher position and you've done a great job. Set it too high and, when you under-achieve, it's back to Shettleston Job Centre.

There are football managers who are very good at telling the press when they're doing well on a low budget, going on an unbeaten run, winning games and getting to the latter stages of cup competitions. Singing our own praises when we were doing well and letting it be known the constraints we were working under was something Alex and I could've done better, but our humility and naivety stopped us doing it. I know one thing, if I ever get back into the coaching/management side of the game, I'll be singing from the rooftops as soon as I get a few wins under my belt and if I don't get that elusive run, I'll be blaming the board.

Remarkably, by the end of the season we had managed to drag the squad up from seventh the previous season to a very respectable third. It was testament to our hard work and maybe even the narrowing of the pitch making things more difficult for the opposition. Being truthful, the football during that season wasn't great and there was a lot of 'percentage' play. We tried to play in the other team's half and get the ball forward early in order to keep it as far away from our goal as possible, but it was the only way we could compensate for the lack of quality in our squad and improve our league position. But, most of all, it gave us rookies some kudos and allowed us to go cap in hand and ask for a bigger budget that would give us a realistic chance of achieving the ultimate ambition of promotion. This second season was going to be our chance to make our mark, we just needed the backing.

Building a winning team and the squad to support the first XI is a skill that few people truly appreciate

194

until they're responsible for doing just that. You need to ensure the players you bring in aren't only capable of playing at the required level but also of doing so consistently while fitting into the team's playing style, buying into what you are trying to achieve and complementing their teammates on and off the park. They need to be of the right character and you need to know you can trust them to do their job each Saturday.

Putting all the bricks in the right places is hard enough at the top of the game when you have blank cheques to wave about, but doing it when you have no money, or next to none, is immeasurably more difficult. We knew there was resentment amongst some fans that the vast majority of the squad drove to Dundee from Glasgow each morning and returned to the west coast after training. What they didn't appreciate was that with the money we were paying and the fact we couldn't offer more security than one-year contracts, insisting that our players had to move to the area would only have further narrowed the range of players we could reasonably attract. Even allowing players to commute sometimes didn't help when competing with teams based in the central belt as even a few quid more wasn't enough compensation for the daily journey for some. We even lost out on players because the journey to Dundee would have wrecked their childcare arrangements. Despite the perceived glamour of the game, footballers have the same commitments and worries as everyone else, but this is sometimes lost on fans.

The purse strings were loosened further in our second and third summers at Dens, but we never had more than the third- or fourth-highest budget in the league and our time was marked by frustration at what might have been in terms of signings.

We were able to hold on to the best out-of-contract players after our first season, with most of them getting a £100 per week wage rise to stay, although we had to push the boat out for big Kevin, who was by now attracting a lot of interest. We needed to add a little more flair into the team as the previous season's brand of safe, percentage football wouldn't get anyone promoted. Livingston were going to take the £50,000 we offered them for Graham Dorrans until West Bromwich Albion stepped in and offered five times that. There was a possibility of taking Leigh Griffiths from Livi's reserves but eventually he signed a new deal for an extra £100 above his YTS wages because he wanted to stay and play with his pals.

Had we got one of them, our squad would have been complete. We knew we were much better than the previous season, but were still missing that one magical player who could win games for us. Expectation is a disease that out-of-work managers have never found a cure for. The fact we had done a decent job in the first season on a shoestring meant that we were now, on the back of a budget increased by 20 per cent, expected to go up.

When you lose out on a player and know what he turned down to sign elsewhere, you have a pretty good idea what other teams around you are paying. We knew Hamilton were paying slightly more than us, but their greatest weapon of all was their plastic pitch. From the start, things went well for us but Accies went on a remarkable season-long unbeaten

196

run at home, conceding only six goals at New Douglas Park during the whole campaign. We took the battle to the second last game of the season but it just wasn't enough and we finished with 69 points, a total that would have won the previous year's championship and the following year's, but this time it wasn't enough and we faced a massive rebuilding job.

Hamilton had also got one over on us in the middle of the season by signing our best striker, Derek Lyle, on a pre-contract agreement. Del was out of contract at the end of the season and Hamilton were able to offer him a deal worth £200 a week more than we could give him. But the real nightmare scenario was us now having a player on our hands who had signed for our promotion rivals. Did we keep him until the end of the season, let him go in January for a nominal fee then have him play against us, or just freeze him out altogether? In fairness, the board stayed out of it for once and allowed us to make the football decision for ourselves, although I felt it was more so they couldn't be held accountable if we made the wrong decision.

As always in football, self-preservation was to the fore. We felt that letting him go was a double negative, strengthening our rivals while weakening us, whereas not playing him at all would have been of no benefit to the club. In the end, the decision was made to keep him till the end of the season and play him as normal. In a playing sense, the decision was the right one as it never affected either individual or team performances, and, even though we were to come up short, we had stuck by our guns and done the right thing.

Lyle wasn't the only departure that summer. The budget was upped again and, although we still weren't up there with St Johnstone and Dunfermline, we felt if we could keep our quality we could challenge. We lost Swankie to St Johnstone, and Scott Robertson and Paul Dixon to Dundee United (which obviously hurt the fans massively), but the biggest loss of all was Kevin MacDonald. The story being peddled to the newspapers was that we had received anything from £500,000 to £750,000 for Kevin but the reality was very different. The club were so desperate to fund the season's budget they accepted just over £300,000 for our best player and the deal was done by the chairman and Burnley boss Owen Coyle behind our backs. It was disappointing that Coyley, who Alex and I'd both known for many years, didn't follow the usual etiquette and let the manager know of his intentions, but I suppose he was just trying to protect his own club to make sure nothing got in the way of the deal as he knew we would try to convince the board to keep him. There was no chance the chairman was going to do anything other than sell that summer, but we would at least have told him to hold out for a lot more money.

The frustration continued when it came to replacing the quality we lost, no more so than when we came within minutes of making the signing of the season. We agreed terms with Robert Snodgrass, who was going to become our highest-paid player (even though the board still wouldn't go to four-figures), largely on account of Snoddy being from Dennistoun and having huge respect for Alex. I had known him from a very young age as he was in my stepson's year at school and we had just about got the deal over the line when Snoddy took a phone call from Gary McAllister at Leeds United. In the space of 10 minutes, the kid had just been offered treble what we had been able to offer and, on the back of a nice signing on fee, he was off to Elland Road. We wished him well, it was an offer he couldn't possibly refuse and it was back to the drawing board for us.

In hindsight we had lost all of our best players and were on a hiding to nothing, but the board were busy telling everyone who wanted to listen that this was the year and the budget had increased so markedly, we HAD to gain promotion. What they failed to mention was that if they'd pushed the boat out and kept our quality, we'd have had a much better chance of rebuilding. Even with an increased budget, promotion was going to be nigh on impossible and, although we went about preparing for that third season with as much determination as the previous two, the writing was already on the wall and had been for some time.

Clubs are always happy to retain your services on their terms. If you are under contract, there will never be any rush to improve it unless you become the target of someone else's advances. Towards the end of our first season at Dundee, and with a year left on our contracts, there had been no talk of extending our initial deals. It would have been nice for my family's sake to know that the club had confidence in us and would be prepared to offer new terms that would give us a bit more stability, but they clearly felt we were still on trial and wouldn't be doing anything until they'd seen how we started the following season.

The phone went in Alex's office and I got up to leave, as I always did when the call seemed to be of a personal nature. An agent was calling to say that the Millwall manager had been sacked and that they were interested in talking to him. With Alex's credentials, links to the club and coaching qualifications he was the perfect fit. He made sure Millwall went through the proper channels and the Dundee board, perhaps sniffing a compensation payment, granted him permission to speak to them.

This was an opportunity we couldn't knock back if it came off. It was what football management was all about; improving yourself, progressing, moving up the ladder. I now had a family to provide for, and it would also mean a bigger salary. At the same time, it was important there would be as little interruption as possible because we didn't want to risk the trust and spirit we had built with the players and destabilise the side. If the interest from Millwall came to nothing it would have undermined our whole season and our attempts to show the board we could be a success. It's something that happens a lot in football – deals are done and managers, players and coaches spoken to without the fans ever knowing anything.

Alex flew down to London after training on the Tuesday, was interviewed for the position the following day (our day off) and was back up for training as normal the next morning. By Friday it had come down to a straight fight between him and Kenny Jackett and, unfortunately for us, it was Kenny's jacket that would be hung up in the gaffer's office at the New Den. The road to the big time was blocked again. Thankfully though, we had made it seem like a normal week and none of the players were any the wiser as we went about our normal match day business on Saturday.

Even though the interest meant our stock within the club rose it was to be seven months before we were called in to the boardroom to discuss new contracts. As it was, we eventually signed new deals in November, but this wasn't about rewarding us for anything; it was purely to ensure the club got suitable compensation should any other vultures come pecking. I was given a wage rise to £35,000 which made a small difference to the monthly family pot, but, crucially, the term length of the contract had changed to 'one year rolling' which effectively meant that for every day I was in employment, my contract had a year left to run. This suited us both as it would mean that if we left to join a bigger club, Dundee would be adequately remunerated and, for me and my family, it meant that if I was sacked then one year's salary was the starting point for compensation negotiations. Or so I thought.

Even as we pushed for promotion there were still signs that all wasn't well behind the scenes and money was clearly still an issue. The club was looking for investment and in March, at an absolutely crucial part of the season, we got the first indication that the club were looking at the possibility of change. Alex was called to a meeting with John Bennett, who was a current Dundee United director and was rumoured to part-own Dens Park. He was clearly a business associate of our chairman Bob Brannan and it became clear the club were courting his knowledge and financial acumen. Alex and I travelled to training together every day which meant I sat bewildered in the car for an hour while he attended his cloak-and-dagger meeting on the outskirts of Dundee. His first words when he jumped back in the car astounded me.

'If he gets in we're fucked!!!' he said.

Alex felt as though he'd just been interviewed for his own job the following season. A vision of the club was outlined and questions were asked as to where we saw the club progressing and how we would go about it. Everything, of course, would be dependent on promotion so at that point it was almost impossible to provide concrete answers. What most concerned Alex was the way Bennett had spent the meeting talking up the achievements of other managers and coaches in the division without mentioning the job we'd done in taking Dundee from mediocrity to stability to challenging for the title. We were battling it out at the top of the league with Hamilton and, while they were attempting to unnerve us by signing our best player, our own board was doing a decent job of putting the wind up us themselves.

They say that the sack is the only inevitable thing in football management, but it still comes as a shock when it happens. The following season was beset with difficulties from the start. We had signed Darren Young and Colin Cameron to build the new side around but both were immediately injured, along with half the rest of the first-team squad. After losing away at Alloa in the Challenge Cup, a competition the club had never particularly bothered about until now, we were given another of those little signs that give you cause for concern. The board refused to pay for an overnight stay before our opening game against Ross

202

County. It was common practice when when playing at Dingwall to travel after training the day before and have a relaxing night at the hotel to prepare properly. We pleaded with them to change their mind and it got to the point where Alex was going to pay for it out of his own pocket before they relented. We won 2-0 against all the odds, but over the coming weeks, the injuries were to take their toll and an inconsistent first 10 games put our jobs under real pressure.

At the start of October we were sitting nine points off top spot, but we knew from murmurings within the club and the inevitable reaction of the home crowd that time wasn't on our side. After a 2-1 defeat in the return fixture with Ross County the reaction from the hospitality section of the main stand was poisonous. It was horrible to experience but, in a strange way, it also makes you want to fight more to prove you can do it. It brings out that masochistic nature that doesn't allow you to lie down.

We vowed to each other to fight on and trained on Monday as normal. Just as we reached the outskirts of Dundee on the journey home we got a phone call to come back to the stadium as chief executive Dave McKinnon wanted to speak to us. We felt sure it would be a rallying call to outline the gravity of the situation and warn of dire consequences if results didn't pick up. After all, were only just over a quarter of the way through the season and, with injuries starting to clear up and no 'vote of confidence' to date, we were sure we'd be given time to turn things around.

There was an eerie feeling as we approached the stadium. Everyone other than the secretary had gone home. Being the leader and the gaffer came

easily to Alex. He was an incredibly strong character and insisted I wait in the car and he'd find out
what was happening. When he re-emerged around
five minutes later, I could just about make out his
silhouette through the murk. His arm was raised,
elbow at shoulder-height and, as he walked back to
the driver's side, I could see him drawing his finger
across his neck in that cut-throat gesture that signi-
fies something is unequivocally over. He jumped in
and confirmed he'd been sacked. 'Fuck off,' was my
rather predictable, unoriginal reply.

'You need to go in and see him, but whatever you
do, don't fuckin' resign, and don't do or say anything
stupid.' I got up, and made my way through the double doors into the manager's office to be greeted by
Dave MacKinnon's hand. It was part-peace offering
and part-sympathy, but little was I to know, the battle
was only just beginning.

I'd finally made it to the exalted position of manager, albeit one prefixed by the word 'caretaker'. At
Stranraer and Albion Rovers I had at the very least
been able to reconcile myself with the possibility of
profiting from someone else's misfortune, but when
your best mate has been sacked the reality of the situation is sobering. The intoxicating power of football
was wearing off and the loneliness of it was cold,
stark and overpowering. I was in my own version of
purgatory.

As a caretaker you're rarely taking over a team on
the up and the role doesn't bring any fulfilment or

worth. You are about to hand over the reins to someone else and, so even if you can somehow come up with a win, the very best it can feel like is chatting up the best looking girl in the disco only for her to go off with someone else. There are generally three types of interim manager – the senior player taking over to try to get the job, the assistant taking over to keep things ticking over and the 'old head' from the coaching set-up not seen as management material, but valued enough to tide the team over whilst the search for a permanent custodian goes on. At Dundee I was caretaker manager for nine days and one game, but in truth it felt like an awful lot longer.

I went into my meeting with Dave MacKinnon extremely angry but determined to remain composed and make sure everything was done by the book. I was informed that the club had decided to make a change as promotion was too important this year and they couldn't afford to fall any further behind in the league. It's at that point you realise that, in football, your past record at a club counts for nothing. No leeway was given for the previous two years of progression under trying circumstances, all that mattered was the here and now. Alex had gone, but as I'd signed my rolling contract less than a year earlier I was expected to hold the fort for the next week while a new manager was sought. It was also mentioned that the board wanted me to apply for Alex's position. I wasn't sure if I'd heard properly. It was almost as if he'd said it because that was part of what you were supposed to say in these circumstances. To be perfectly honest, I thought he'd a fucking cheek even suggesting it.

Alex had brought me in and given me this opportunity and our friendship superseded any ambition I may have had to be a manager in my own right. Throughout my career I'd tried to behave with as much dignity and respect as is possible in football and I wasn't going to give that up now. I would take the first-team for the next week with the help of our youth coach, Paul Ritchie. I was to be caretaker manager until I felt the swing of the Grim Reaper's scythe. As long as I played everything by the book and never gave the club the opportunity to accuse me of breaking the terms of my contract I could preserve my legal position before being shunted out of the door when the new manager came in. At that point the inevitable fight for compensation would be triggered.

Under different circumstances I wanted to be in charge, standing in the firing line and making the decisions. I didn't want the job, not even temporarily, but I'd no choice and took it with Alex's blessing. Maybe it was a fault in me that I never quite had that ruthlessness to succeed at all costs, to do whatever it takes to get on if that meant shafting people on the way. I couldn't sleep at night anyway so what difference would it make if I was a horrible bastard with no morals? But I couldn't and would rather not sleep for the right reasons. Throughout the nine days of my janitorial duties I made it clear that I would keep my current desk and not use the manager's office. It was the least I could do for someone who had shown tremendous loyalty in appointing me in the first place.

One of the most overwhelming things about being caretaker is the underwhelming nature of it. I no longer wanted to be there. My friend and gaffer had

206

gone and the truth was I would rather have gone with him there and then, but I had a job to do and, regardless of how I felt, I would do the best I could for the players.

I put the brave face paint on and we prepared as usual for the next game, away at Morton. I had little option to change the team because our squad was depleted by injury and there was few options to change things tactically. As assistants we do everything required of the manager, we support team selections and everything the manager does. If I had made six changes and tried to play a different way that would have made me a fraud. Why would I not have suggested to Alex before now that we should do that? Do clubs think that we had some magic formula that we had been keeping secret from the manager?

As it was I did do one thing slightly differently pre-match. I could sense a flatness among the players and felt that, under the circumstances, we needed to start the game brightly. Cappielow is a small ground and the away dressing room is one of the smallest in the country. Cramped and cold with a massage bench in the middle, there was no room for a push-up never mind an impromptu First Division 'Haka' but I gathered the team round in a circle and brought them to boiling point running on the spot before they headed out. It was frenzied, loud and energetic and, you know what, it worked...for 20 minutes. I got a tune out of them, I really did, but as the game settled and a team already lacking in confidence lost a goal, I could see the shoulders dropping. At that point I'm not sure the best motivational coach on the planet could've got them going again. They were devoid of ideas and the spark had gone. We went on to lose 2-0 and my foray into the world of management was over.

I was a disconsolate figure when interviewed by the press afterwards. I got a sympathetic ear as they knew I didn't want to be in front of them under those circumstances, but I at least owed the players and the club that. Win, lose or draw, I was leaving the building but I couldn't walk away from my responsibility and refuse to talk to the media.

After training on Monday, Dave MacKinnon informed me the club had appointed Jocky Scott as manager and he'd be bringing in his own staff, which was an entirely normal, acceptable practice. I was given the opportunity to come back the next day to remove all my belongings and say my goodbyes. Football has no real place for sentiment and I didn't particularly want to make any sort of scene. Neither did I want to show any sign of weakness, so I would quietly say goodbye to anyone who was still around that afternoon and wish everyone luck. I'd enjoyed my time at the club and, although frustrated at not being given a little more time to turn things around, there was no real cause for resentment at that point. Dave and I spoke briefly about the contract situation and I was told it was in the hands of the lawyers and contact would be maintained over the next few days in the hope of getting things sorted. I took that to mean there would be amicable dialogue and we would come to a compromise agreement fairly quickly and responsibly. How wrong I was.

∗

Unemployment very quickly eats up everything. It eats up your self-esteem, it eats up your pride, and it definitely eats up your cash. You become a doormat that people have to step over to get about the house you rattle around in day after day. I was on the dole for six months after I left Dundee and they were without a doubt the worst six months of my life. I was a working guy and I needed to provide for my family.

On the back of signing that new contract less than a year previously, we felt we had enough security for Samantha to go back to college and train as a beauty therapist. We were making plans for the future and the one-year rolling contract offered the stability of the compensation to fall back on should the worst happen. I should have known better than to think ahead. Football rarely gave me a break and this was to be no different, but that wasn't how I felt the day after I left Dens.

I woke up the next morning a free man, free from football and free from the biting pressure that comes with it. There was no relief, only disappointment that we had failed to finish the job after a tough two-and-a-half years. I had a few 'rainy day' grand in the bank and when I say a few I mean only enough to keep the family ticking over for a couple of months and supplement my £112 a week unemployment benefit without affecting Samantha's bursary. It's strange how, in times of adversity, small mercies can seem like gifts from God. It wasn't as if I had any extra cash trousered away in a Swiss bank account that no one knew about. This was the reality, we would be living off the state and my minimal savings.

We had a holiday booked for the end of May, but that was still eight months away so I was sure I would have a new job by then or at least Dundee would have paid up on the remainder of my contract. I got a letter from the club to say that they were terminating my contract as of that final Monday and from that point on there was no further correspondence. No mention of the legalities, no talk about wages and no foreseeable agreement on how much they would pay me for my remaining year. And that was it. From that day forward, they stopped paying me.

As far as I was concerned, our contracts were watertight and Alex's lawyer had confirmed as much. While there was absolutely no question the club were in breach of contract, I was in for a long, drawn-out battle as they tried to renege on what they were due. Their stance was that the contract was in fact a year's rolling, but only on their terms and they had exercised their right not to continue it. It's what clubs in Scotland do, they make you suffer by stopping your wages and then hope you will accept a reduced compensation package because most people in Scottish football don't have that nest egg to fall back on.

I put the phone down and immediately called the PFA and instructed the lawyer to pursue an unfair dismissal case. case. In situations like this clubs never have a leg to stand on, but hope you take another job before the case is called, which usually takes up to a year, so your earnings can be deducted from any final compensation payment. It's a disgusting practice and one carried out with no regard for the hardship the individual or his family may be going through in the meantime. All they're interested in is starving you of cash until you come back with the begging bowl and accept much less than you're due just so you can support your family. I called Dave back and asked him outright what was his perception of what 'one year rolling' meant. His answer was unequivocal. 'My understanding was that for every day you were in employment, your contract still had a year to run.' I made sure I recorded that part of the conversation and I now had the evidence to prove my case, provided I could sit it out in the meantime.

Unemployment bleeds every ounce of decency you have as you make the fortnightly visit to hell. It would take every piece of resolve I had not to buckle and accept a reduced payment. After three months it was becoming increasingly tough. There was no real prospect of returning to the game and I had to keep things together for the family. The money was running out and Dundee had made it clear they were going to court so I was in it for the long haul. I put a brave face on things, continuing to do the same things I always had, and not letting Samantha or the kids know how difficult things were.

I'd find the money from somewhere, borrowing from my best friends to keep things ticking over and all the while leading the soul-destroying daily 'Jeremy Kyle' existence of the destitute. We'd go to all the same places and everyone thought I was okay, the kids would get everything they needed and we'd all dress the same and look the part, but inside I was hurting. I couldn't let anyone see it. Until now, my two best pals were the only people who knew I borrowed money to keep things ticking over. I told Samantha

I got a loan from the bank and that the buroo money would cover it and I just pretended to my Mum and Dad that I'd saved enough over the years to keep us going. I was really struggling to keep things going and, after six months, I needed to find a job. The PFA had been great with their support and they provided lawyers as part of the union subsidies, but I really needed the court hearing date to be finalised so we could bring things to a head.

I had offers to go back into part-time youth coaching, but training two nights a week and spending Sundays away at Elgin or Cowdenbeath wasn't appealing enough for the £50 per week expenses that would be deducted from my dole money. A date was finally set for the hearing but it fell on the Monday before we were due to fly home from our holiday. It would mean that if we couldn't come to any sort of agreement (the hearing was still three months away) I'd have to get on a plane and fly back early. My lawyer assured me our case was watertight but, as we approached holiday time, it was clear we were still miles away from coming to an agreement.

Whilst I was looking to take Dundee for every penny I was due I was also keen to avoid a court date. However, at that point we were just too far apart and it was looking more and more likely I'd be flying home early. With no agreement in sight, I borrowed some more cash from my pals in shining armour, so that we could have a nice holiday without my family worrying about what we could and couldn't spend. I had put them in this mess by chasing MY dream, just as I always had done, and felt I needed to protect them from the truth. Thankfully they were never fully aware of how serious things had been for the last few months as I juggled bills, cash, loans and overdrafts to make sure no one in my family suffered.

All Samantha knew was that enough money was going into the accounts at the end of the month to cover what we needed. There were cutbacks, but as long as the kids didn't suffer then I'd have done my job as a father. Some would argue that by getting them into this position in the first place I hadn't done a particularly good job of it, but we had always lived within our means and, ultimately, it was the club who were in the wrong.

Minimal dialogue between the legal minds continued and I boarded the plane not knowing whether I'd be forced to return early to sit in on the tribunal. Three days in and my mobile rang. Dundee were getting closer to our previously discussed settlement figure and, now the game of brinkmanship had started, I was determined not to back down. I wasn't going through nine months of hell to settle for anything less than I felt I was due. It became clear that Dundee didn't want to go all the way to court and incur extensive legal costs as well as risking a full and final settlement.

You know that asshole at the pool, with the phone glued to his ear as he talks to his hotshot lawyer, while his wife/partner/girlfriend/lover/mistress glares angrily and begs him to put it away with her stare without saying anything? Well, that was me, and that was the defining feature of my family holiday that year. I made a trip to the airport to check what flights would make sure I was in Scotland for the tribunal's scheduled Monday morning 9am start. The phone calls continued and, as the weekend drew nearer, we got closer to an agreement.

All the while, Samantha was urging me to give in and just enjoy the holiday but I couldn't. I held on until the Friday afternoon, when my lawyer advised that to continue now may end up being detrimental and we reached a settlement three days before we were due to go to court. Three fucking days!!! Had they come to me the day after I was sacked, I would have settled for half the amount I was now to receive but the fact my wages were stopped without any consideration for my family or my circumstances, meant I went all-out. I was disgusted at the way they had attempted to get out of paying me after I'd been nothing less than a model employee.

The relief was palpable and I was proud I'd managed to stick it out. I looked at Samantha and the kids and smiled, relieved that we'd be able to get on with a proper family life again without any more stress. Except that I hadn't quite stopped putting them through the wringer to feed my addiction and ego just yet.

A Moth to a Flame
2008-2014

Clyde
Notts County
Celtic Nation

No management team gets everything right. Even the best have to reflect upon signings that didn't work out, games that were approached the wrong way or any one of the countless other decisions that will have cost them sleep at some point. Our time at Dundee was no different. Mistakes were made, but we were a young team working with at least one hand tied behind our back most of the time and I still feel Alex should have been given more time to recover the situation given how close we'd run Hamilton the year before.

Painfully, the final game of that season saw Hamilton visit Dens the week after clinching the league. They had some great players including James McArthur and James McCarthy, who've attracted more than £15 million in transfer fees between them since then, so I can never say we would've won the league had Hamilton played on grass. I'm adamant, however, that without the advantage the plastic pitch gave them, we would have gone into that final game with a chance of still going up. Who knows what would have happened in that AstroTurf-free parallel universe but in this one I was back at New Douglas Park, not as a coach or as a manager, but as a labourer maintaining the surface that was at least a contributing factor in my sacking and subsequent unemployment. Me and irony were not best pals at this point.

My compensation from Dundee allowed me to repay the mates who'd seen me through the dark nine months that followed my sacking and to come off Jobseeker's Allowance. Now I had to find myself a job in the real world. Barring the six weeks after losing my job at Airdrie, this was the first time I'd been out of football in 22 years. It was daunting, but I had a family to support and I'd long since learned that football didn't owe me a living.

Half my settlement went towards paying off loans, credit cards and my overdraft. The other half would be my next 'rainy day' savings account, ready and waiting for the next time I got the sack. That's the nature of football at my level. Get a job, get the sack, make the savings last until you get the next one and on and on the whole merry-go-round goes. Throughout my playing career I was signed by clubs in adversity or financial trouble and my coaching career was refusing to give me a break either. I was helping out with a small coaching group in the summer holidays at Petershill Park in Glasgow, just to keep things ticking over until something else came up. Even though there are hundreds of good, even very good, coaches out of work, you still believe the phone will ring and save you from having to get a real job. But a real job it was to be.

I bumped into my old team-mate Brian Hamilton, who now had his own company supplying, laying and maintaining AstroTurf gardens and 3G pitches. When he offered me a labouring job I wasn't in a position to say no, so for the next year I grafted away

218

laying the artificial grass that had been my nemesis. It was tough, back-breaking work in all weathers and the newly acquired, compensation-laden rainy day fund was still dipped into more times than a drunk husband's pockets. The physical aspect of the work was tough, but fulfilling. For a working-class man there are few better feelings than carting a wheelbarrow, digging trenches and sweating buckets in order to put food on your family's table (although running about a football pitch was certainly one), but the mental side of the job was much more demanding. In fact it was demoralising. I was working with guys who had hammered, screwed and drilled their way through their lives. They were used to it, but I was used to being a footballer.

We'd go to lay the synthetic grass in gardens, football grounds and public parks and the interrogations would start.

'Didn't you used to play for Hibs?'

'What happened at Dundee?'

'How'd you end up doing this?'

'No chance of getting back in to football?'

Like when I scuttled into the Job Centre, I was probably recognised a lot less than it seemed at the time, but I would sometimes work with a hard hat on in the height of summer and dip my head into an unnatural position if I was going to work on a pitch where I thought people might know me. I enjoyed the physical side of the work, but I hated the job itself because it put me in a position where I had to admit that I was an outcast, no longer a part of football.

The visits to New Douglas Park were particularly

tortuous. Everyone at the club was great because football can be all camaraderie and concern at times, but underneath the handshakes from manager Billy Reid and the players, I knew they were stifling the smugness and contempt that said 'look where you are now and look where we are'. No one ever said it out loud, but I was among football people and knew that's what they would be thinking. And yet I still wanted to be a football person more than anything.

We were on the way back from a job in Aberdeen when the phone rang to offer me my way back in. John 'Cowboy' McCormack had just been given the manager's job at Clyde and was looking for an assistant. We'd had some minor dealings over the years, but the fact we were relative strangers wasn't my main concern. The remit was to keep them up, but, with the club in turmoil and the team on its arse, it seemed a thankless task. There was no problem with Brian so it came down to whether or not I felt I could make a difference and whether there were any prospects at all of us making progress that would lead to a decent job higher up the ladder.

I used the extra £150 (less tax) per week that would be coming into the house to sell the offer to Samantha, but I knew she wouldn't stand in my way, even if she would rather I turned the job down so the kids would see more of me. Money was found for Cowboy to bring in four or five players on loan, but the kids we had at our disposal just weren't up to it and it quickly became apparent that Clyde were very unlikely to stay up. The standard of training from the players was poor and it was being transferred to matches where we couldn't even buy a win.

As an assistant manager you have to be many things, but the most important thing from the manager's point of view is that he can trust you to do whatever is required at any time. Juggling the whims, needs, wants and quirks of 22 egotistical grown men is one of the main causes of managerial insomnia so the one person you need to know will never let you down is your assistant.

There are huge differences in the resources available to coaching staff at the top level, but that principle remains the same. In my experience you have to make the manager's job an easier one, whether he asks you to do a lot (as some do) or a little. But, above all, the relationship with the players is essential. The manager doesn't have to be liked, but the assistant does. He has to be a go-between, a counsellor, a good coach, a friend and a leader.

As an assistant manager you have to be incredibly subservient at times. I was no shrinking violet and the players knew that I didn't tolerate non-triers, but everyone got a break now and then if they deserved it. However, I also knew that if I made a mistake or said something out of turn I could be cut down in front of the players, purely for effect. This would serve as a reminder that no one was safe from the manager's wrath and it certainly kept the players on their toes. And me on mine.

John was a different manager to those I'd experienced before, being very much old school. He was a motivator, encouraging, cajoling and growling at players in equal measure in order to get what he could from them, but the young players in particular weren't responding to it. Through all this I felt lost. I was a coach, but I wasn't doing any coaching. Although we worked on passing, crossing, finishing and shooting – all of which were unquestionably required as we couldn't manufacture a goal from open play – with John organising and taking every session I felt like a spare part.

As a manager you have every right to manage as you see fit, but I found it difficult not getting my hands dirty, so to speak. I loved coaching, getting in among the players, teaching them and putting them in the right place. John felt the players weren't up to retaining the information, that it would only confuse them, and that we needed to get the best out of them in other ways, but I believed the young lads needed guidance and help.

In my five months at Clyde, I think I was in charge of one session and even that turned into a disaster as I set the bar too high with what I demanded of them. I'd played and coached at this level before and knew what players should be capable of. It was a straightforward conditioned game, the sort of thing professional footballers up and down the country do week in, week out. You set up two teams of eight and certain parts of the pitch are zoned off. Players can move from zone to zone, but only if certain conditions, like a certain amount of passes reached, or a specific, key player gaining possession, are met. It can be used to work on all manner of strengths and weaknesses in a team. Unfortunately for us, it highlighted a serious lack of technical ability and knowledge of the game.

They ended up running into each other and shooting into the wrong end as the defenders attacked and the attackers defended. Maybe Cowboy was right after all, but I thought it was at least worth giving them the opportunity to learn a bit more about the game. The fact they couldn't process what I saw as simple information wasn't a good sign. As far as I could see, this team was only going one way, and that was down.

I continued to work as hard as I could, doing exactly as John required, which meant being a balls, bibs and cones man – one of those lapdog coaches who sets up pitches and take down goals at the gaffer's behest. Cowboy had given me an opportunity to get back in the game and I at least owed him that. My personal pride and conscientious nature wouldn't have allowed me to be anything other than loyal to the big man, but I was frustrated and felt I had much more to offer than that.

Off the pitch, I'd never felt more tired. When I started playing part-time, I had a comfortable day job in the college, but now I was doing tough, manual labour and leaving the house at 6.30am every day. I was shattered, racing about all over Scotland to shovel tons of sand and stone before heading to training twice a week. If there was a midweek away game I might not get home before midnight. I didn't see the kids three days each week as I was out to work before they were up and they were back in bed before I returned. Football wasn't meant to be like this. I owed Brian a lot as he'd given me a job when I was on my arse, but the work was really starting to affect me.

The £111 a week after tax from Clyde hardly

seemed worth the extra sacrifices but, as I suspected, it wasn't to last too long anyway. Clyde were officially relegated about a month before the season's end but our tenure had been brought to an end a couple of weeks before that when the position at the bottom became irretrievable. I was sacked, out of the game again. I had no choice but to stick with a job I was extremely grateful for, but disliked passionately, in order to provide for the children I was hardly seeing.

Brian could have employed anyone he pleased, but he knew he could trust me to keep control of the boys and look after the equipment. By now he'd put me into a supervisory role on sites. Most of the workers had worked in construction for a long time and their knowledge of ground conditions and requirements was far greater than mine. I knew they resented the fact an outsider was in charge of them, but Brian needed someone who would be disciplined enough to make sure the boys were on time and didn't mess about whilst getting the jobs completed to a high standard. I suppose it was a bit like being assistant manager. I couldn't afford a family summer holiday which meant I'd worked from June 2009 right through to the following October without a break. I was shattered, but there was also the faintest sign of light at the end of the tunnel.

By now, Alex was working at MK Dons and this led to me occasionally doing a bit of scouting for them in Scotland. I knew most of the players they'd been recommended already, but it was good to get back out around the grounds again, taking in matches and lapping up the freebies. Now that I was representing an English team as a scout, I was deemed important enough to merit lounge access to boost to my ego, which was by now as fragile as my legs had been towards the end of my playing days. I was desperate to find a way back in for real and, as it turned out, my big break was just round the corner.

This wasn't a big break like my Dundee big break, you understand. This was my Paul Ince big break. That's right, THE Paul Ince. In my head I was already jumping ahead to the day when some keen-but-cursed young coach was talking about how he came to work under THE Davie Farrell.

Incey and Alex had been team-mates at Wolves and Paul took him to MK Dons as a scout and youth coach. When Incey left for Notts County in October 2010 and his assistant took on the vacant hot seat in Milton Keynes, Alex went with him to Meadow Lane as his new number two. They'd call me on the way back from training to discuss who was available in Scotland. 'What's such and such like?', 'there's a left-back at Aberdeen, could he play in League One?' or 'how much would he cost us?' The subject would then inevitably get round to Celtic and Rangers and Incey would be listening intently on loudspeaker in his Jag, roaring with laughter at Alex and I tearing each other (and each other's clubs) to pieces, before deciding he wanted some of the action and throwing his Cockney tuppence-worth in.

Alex and I had spoken almost every day for over 30 years so I thought nothing of it when my mobile told me he was calling again as I sat in the car outside

Samantha's mum's place in Riddrie one evening. By the time the call ended I was shaking with adrenaline and skipping up the path to the house.

There was a vacancy for a first-team coach at Notts County. There was someone in place at the club, but Incey wanted to build a team he knew he could trust and there was no question the guy would be moved on, just as I had been at Dundee. They had discussed some options and then my name had been thrown into the ring. Alex explained that Paul had liked the way I spoke about players and could tell I had a good knowledge of the game, but the biggest thing of all was that he could see the bond between Alex and me, which would ensure he had two trusted lieutenants should things work out. Someone as high-profile as Paul Ince couldn't just go on Alex's recommendation and his own gut instinct so I was invited down so he could see how I worked in person. It was the first time I'd ever heard of anyone going on trial as a coach!

I went in to make the inevitable plea and explain that, this time, this really was my chance. I'd always sold the coaching to Samantha on the premise that one job could change our lives – the great opportunity, the financial jackpot. Moving up the ladder from Stranraer straight to the San Siro was pie in the sky, but this was time it was different. This was Paul Ince, for fuck's sake. Of Liverpool, Man Utd and Inter Milan fame. England captain and Premier League winner. A veteran of World Cups and European Championships. If I could just go down there and prove myself and hang on to the coat-tails of someone with that sort of reputation and kudos, surely we'd get a crack at the big time. I was getting so carried away with it all that, as usual, I hadn't even thought about the consequences.

I would be lucky to see Sam and the kids once a week and the money would have to be enough to compensate for those sacrifices, but in my heart of hearts nothing would stop me. Samantha encouraged me at all times through the years and throughout all the sackings and back stabbings. She knew how much I wanted to be a success and work at the highest level. And now that I had a family I wanted to provide a wonderful lifestyle for them.

The situation was complicated by the fact she was only halfway through her second year at college but, just like every other time when I decided that football was to come first, she'd have to keep the home together. People always talk about the difficulties of working away from home but those left behind have it so much tougher. Keeping the peace with the kids, picking them up, doing the school runs and the after-school clubs, humouring them, educating them and keeping them busy and out of trouble as well as organising a home. I would only be coaching footballers.

I was introduced to the players, who were told I was to be coming in to help for a few weeks. I took in the match on Saturday, a comfortable 2-0 home win against Gateshead in the FA Cup, and then trained with the players the following week in preparation for an away game at Exeter. I was only supposed to be staying until the Friday, so it was important I made a strong impression that week. I knew the players wouldn't know me, but that a quick Google would tell them I was Alex's mate, so I had to show them I was capable, knowledgeable and affable, and wasn't just there because of nepotism. I had to be strong and make sure that if anyone questioned my methods I would respond and prove myself to be right. It was a fine balancing act, but I had to get across an element of authority without being overbearing or there would be the usual 'Who the fuck does he think he is?' comments.

Footballers are very quick to seize on weakness. It's important that you are prepared from a technical point of view, but the relationship you have with the players is just as important. Respect will buy you time and it's rarely afforded to those coaches who are disliked. Incey was terrific with me, the most down-to-earth millionaire I've ever met. Football brings people together regardless of health or wealth. Alex had told me he was a football nut who didn't just watch every game, but studied the shapes, formations and team selections – a man after my own heart.

We had lost at Exeter, but my main concern was the fact it was now 10 days since I'd gone down to Nottingham and I needed to know where I stood. I spoke to Alex and he told me the best time to get Incey was during Monday's live TV game when we could have a drink and go through the tactics in the match. The plan was obviously to pounce after getting him half-pissed, but a spanner was thrown in the works when I found out he enjoyed a glass of Sancerre. I'd never even heard of Sancerre, never mind paid for one. Thankfully I found out that it wasn't TOO expensive as he allowed me to buy him ONE glass, although he generally bought a bottle. They never sold it in The

228

Crown, that's for sure. Being honest, I was a little awestruck. Paul was charismatic and had a tremendous presence and, being an English legend, people in the bar would talk, point and ask to have their photo taken with him. It was surreal but on another level it felt very natural to me as it was just two football men talking about their passion. Thinking about it in those terms helped prevent me from looking like a gobsmacked schoolboy in the presence of the sixth-year girl with the biggest chest.

Finally the elephant in the room had to be addressed. 'Can you let me know what's happening? I need to find out so I can let the family know and go back to my job next week if it's not going to work out.'

There was an awkward silence as I waited on his response. The whole future of my family could hang on his answer.

'What you talking about? I thought you already knew.'

'Knew what?'

'I've told the chief executive to sort you out. Go and see him in the morning. I made my mind up last Tuesday when you took that session and then we had a chat with the players afterwards about tactics. I thought you knew then.'

I was screaming 'YOU MIGHT'VE FUCKIN' TOLD ME!' in my head but more than anything I was ecstatic. It was typical of an experienced manager to keep me on my toes and not jump into a rash decision, especially when I was in no position to push for an early answer.

I thanked Paul while continuing to play it cool. This was my opportunity and I had to make it look like being in the presence of big names came naturally to me as anything else would have been seen as a weakness. I was in, and nothing could take that away from me. Well, not yet anyway.

It quickly became apparent that there is a huge difference between a club struggling financially in Scotland and one on its knees in England's third tier. Notts County were, in relative terms, in turmoil, but they still had everything they needed and more. Two physios, a masseuse, conditioning coach, nutritionist, kit man, video analyst and sports scientist – it was a back-up team worthy of a top side, never mind one struggling in the bottom four places of League One. Clubs outside the Premier League complain bitterly about the lack of TV money that trickles down the divisions but they absolutely coin it in compared to Scottish Premiership clubs.

It was for that reason that I was slightly disappointed when I went to see the chief executive the morning after my chat with Incey and was told my wages would be £30,000 a year. I was giving up a lot by leaving home and I knew the demands of the job meant I couldn't even guarantee that I'd be able to travel back up the road once a week to see my family. But, once again, I was in no position to haggle.

The club was very unstable as it recovered from a failed takeover bid and having been taken to the brink of bankruptcy by the ill-fated reign of former

England boss Sven Goran Eriksson, one of its eight managers in the previous two years. For me, all this meant I certainly wouldn't be making my fortune, especially when the cost of travelling up and down from Glasgow once a week (if I was lucky) was factored in. Indeed, there were times when that old rainy day account was dipped into again. I couldn't let Samantha know we were short, that I'd gone all the way down there and we were still no better off. How could I possibly justify upping sticks and leaving her to pick up the pieces and still be struggling financially? I couldn't, so as long as the bills were being paid somehow, I put all thoughts of anything other than what a great opportunity this was to one side.

I threw myself into the job and got to know everyone at the club, the players and, more importantly, the opposition. I locked myself away for hours with a laptop, watching DVDs and online footage of every team in the league. With Alex having worked at MK Dons he had a good knowledge of the division but if Incey asked a question about a player, manager, formation or system, I wanted him to know that I had the answer. Alex and I drove all over the country watching games. Carlisle, Exeter, Peterborough, Rochdale and other grounds I'd only read about or seen on the Football League Show. By the end of that first month, I knew about League One alright. If I was going to fail it wouldn't be through lack of application.

We changed the style of play and got the side organised, playing higher up the pitch and narrower. The result was that we became much more difficult to beat and our hard work began to pay dividends. We won five of our next six games and lost only two goals in the process, which was particularly pleasing to me as it showed the work I'd done to try to get County defending like a proper team was working.

All the while there were little signs that things still weren't right. This was a dressing room the likes of which I'd never experienced before, and Paul and Alex had been warned by people in the game not to touch the job. The board were notorious for being trigger happy, continually hiring and firing and readying the axe again as soon as the short-term reaction that a new boss sometimes gets from the players wore off. As a coach and manager you always back yourself to be able to turn things around at a club, but the lack of stability over the previous few years had allowed the players to obtain an incredible amount of influence.

I've always been of the belief that if you are the captain of a ship you should never allow the crew to run it. Unfortunately at Notts, not only were the players running it, they were also running it into the ground. It was too early in our reign for us to have lost the dressing room, but it was clear that many of the other managers who had been in our position had. There were players who had been given three-year contracts under Eriksson who were playing out the last season on money that was much, much more than they deserved given their ability. The result was players sitting on their contracts because they knew no-one would match their wages, which meant a tight budget being squeezed further by players unable to contribute to getting the club out of its situation. That restricted the manoeuvring open to any incoming manager but the board did free up some cash for Paul to bring in some loan players. Thomas

Ince and Stephen Darby from Liverpool, Alan Judge from Blackburn, Lee Miller from Middlesbrough and Conor Clifford from Chelsea would ensure we had some quality at our disposal and, as well as that decent run in the league, we had an FA Cup tie away at Sunderland to look forward to.

I spoke earlier about how big teams should always beat wee teams if they prepare properly, but it was clear that Sunderland weren't doing that and had taken it for granted they would beat us. The gaffer and Steve Bruce were great friends from their time at Old Trafford and we were invited to stop off at the Stadium of Light for our dinner the night before the game. It was a nice gesture, but I felt they were being over-friendly and weren't treating the big FA Cup tie too seriously. Clearly, playing a team from two divisions below wasn't as important to them as the prospect of a Premiership scalp was to us. It was all too civil for me and, when we saw their team sheet the next day, we knew we had a chance. They were resting players whereas we were gritty, organised and determined. We beat the Mackem millionaires 2-1. Things couldn't get better, it seemed. Then they did.

Twenty-four years after my Old Trafford 'debut' I was back in Manchester and back in the dugout – or rather 'technical area' – as my side faced one of the biggest clubs in England. It was City and not United we were squaring up to this time and the stadium we played at wasn't so much as a blot of ink from an architect's pen back then. And, make no mistake about it, we had earned our shot at the big time.

As we waited on the draw the day after we knocked Sunderland out, there was huge anticipation around the club. I'd heard all about the magic and the prestige of the FA Cup, this time I was experiencing it. The small club awaiting their fate or their reward, whatever way the balls were to go, and then it happened – Notts County at home to... Manchester City!!! The highest-profile tie we could've hoped for.

It was a challenge that I, as a coach, could only have dreamt of before and, like all challenges throughout my career, it was one I would relish. Alex and I formulated a tactical plan and then put our strategy to Incey. We would press them high up the pitch in a 4-3-3 formation when Joe Hart had the ball as this would stop them playing to their strengths and building from the back. We couldn't go toe-to-toe with them as they had much better players than us so we would drop back to a 4-5-1 as they gained possession to give us the opportunity to frustrate them and keep it at 0-0 for as long as possible.

Set pieces would be key. As we were unlikely to break them down from open play, our best chance of scoring probably came from a dead ball. Manchester City, unlike Sunderland, didn't underestimate us. They started most of their big stars, with the exception of David Silva. Our game plan couldn't have gone any better and, with 15 minutes gone in the second half, we got a corner. Our midfielder Neal Bishop made a near-post run and glanced a header straight into the roof of Joe Hart's net. Incredibly, we had taken the lead.

My family were all there to witness that wonderful moment. My Dad, who had watched me in reserve

234

games from Brechin to Berwick, had a smile as wide as the Clyde as I looked up at him, sitting only six rows from me in the main stand. I'm sure he was incredibly proud to see me punching my weight among the millionaires but, typically, a slight frown came over his face and he immediately brought me back down to earth by instructing me to concentrate on the game.

Unfortunately we couldn't hold on. David Silva was sent into the fray as soon as we scored and, for 20 minutes, we couldn't get near City's insurance policy as he popped the ball about and probed from positions our formation couldn't handle. Eventually he slipped a pass into the path of Micah Richards who smashed it across the face of the goal for Edin Dzeko to tap in. We had come within seven minutes of another giant killing, but at least we had earned a replay. I had never felt a greater sense of personal achievement than that day because the game plan, the blueprint that Alex and I had pored over and planned to every last detail, had been applied to the letter and worked. It was my tactical pinnacle, my coaching utopia.

The replay at Eastlands, as it was known then, was an incredible experience. We knew we would struggle to impose ourselves as much as we did at Meadow Lane, when everything was in our favour; from a hostile crowd to the tight, old-school stadium and the momentum of an FA Cup giant-killing in the previous round. But this was different, this was their gaff, and what a place it was. From the moment our coach made its way down the underground tunnel that eventually led to the dressing room area, the place oozed Arabian dirham. It was a five-star hotel disguised as a football stadium.

235

The changing area itself was huge, with a blue, synthetic floor and individual lockers above solid benches. The traditional physio's bench was pristine, hydraulic, and housed in a separate medical area at the end of the changing room. It had a different postcode to where I was getting changed. I walked out to the office area to drop off some tickets for the players' families (in all honesty I was being nosey and wanted to have a look at the place) and as you walked through the corridors everything was tiled, finished and trimmed in Man City blue and what seemed like gold. Everything gleamed and was fitted out to the highest standard. They even had a Starbucks for staff within the stadium's administration area. All in all, it was a far cry from Cliftonhill.

Once again our game plan revolved around making things difficult for our millionaire opponents, keeping it scoreless for as long as possible and hoping we could nick the first goal at some point and hold on. After around 15 minutes we broke up the park and, following a terrific move, we struck the post at the end where our 3,500 fans were. It was to be our only chance of the game and a 5-0 drubbing followed.

Once they had scored the first goal, it was about damage limitation as they used a combination of momentum, relief and supreme confidence to toy with us. As a coach, it was both tortuous and a joy to watch. These were world-class footballers at the top level, displaying technique and football of the highest order.

After the game we made our way into the area reserved for manager's guests. Traditionally, you

236

make your way to the opposition gaffer's office after a game and share a beer or two. At City, they had a separate suite with Chesterfield furniture and the best of everything. The duration of the hospitality depends on how much the participants like each other and, sometimes, the result, but I wasn't going to pass up these particular vol-au-vents for anything. Incey, though, had decided to give it a miss. City manager Roberto Mancini had snubbed him at Meadow Lane when he never bothered to come in to his office after the game. Paul had bought a nice bottle of wine for them to share, none of that Sancerre Leibfraumilch, but Mancini decided he had better things to do.

I tried to convince Paul to come in and not let Mancini ruffle him, but he wasn't having it. 'Fuck him,' was his reply to me. I shouldn't have offered my opinion as it wasn't my place as first-team coach, but I held him in such high regard that I would have loved to have seen him taking the credit he was due from the City staff that included old friends and associates of his like David Platt and Brian Kidd. Paul was a principled man and he felt Mancini was taking the piss by not turning up after the first game so wouldn't be moved. I respected that, but I wasn't going to miss the opportunity myself and we sat talking football for around 20 minutes, international playing and coaching legends and me, who had been hiding my face at Shettleston Job Centre not so long ago. I was in heaven, throwing in the odd contribution and bouncing off Alex, who was more accustomed to such esteemed company having played in the Premier League for many years.

That FA Cup run was the undoubted highlight

of my coaching career but, as I should really have known by then, the inevitable kick in the teeth was only just around the corner.

It's a strange quirk of football, sports in general I suppose, that short-term success often makes ultimate failure more likely. The club had made approximately £750,000 from the cup run, but the board, having witnessed an improvement in the team's performance, were satisfied there was no need to push the boat out and bring in more quality. Our good form in the league and our FA Cup exploits helped encourage the parent clubs of our loanees to recall their players and, as those who had been discarded a few months earlier came back into the reckoning one-by-one, we had a major problem on our hands.

This group was starting to create mayhem. According to them, the lunches weren't good enough, the training was shite, the gym facilities were falling to bits and the double sessions were a joke. When footballers aren't playing, the slightest issue becomes a crisis whether the team is winning or not. When you get a group like that it can very quickly become an inoperable cancer and we now had to rely on players who no longer respected us or had any interest in playing for us. Results started to dip and they started to drag everyone down with their negativity. We were on the way to losing the dressing room.

The most difficult times for a manager are usually during the early months of a reign where authority needs to be stamped and respect gained. Training must be bright, disciplined and enjoyable during this crucial period and we had managed to get that. Paul immediately gained the respect of the players from his stature alone. He made it clear he wanted Alex and I to deal with the players as much as possible and leave the board and off-field issues to him.

The three of us would control the playing side. We'd put together the drills and the theme for the day's training and the gaffer would just give us a nod in the morning or change whatever he felt was required. We made sure everything was right for him and dealt with everything, whether it was discipline, bus times, lunch issues, player meetings, arguments, staff issues. Players must know immediately that you're not to be messed with. It meant that we had to deal with occasional confrontation, when players would try to get out of training due to a niggle (or after a night out), but we had no issue with standing up to them. If players step out of line, either on or off the pitch, they must know it won't be tolerated. This is where respect is gained and trust formed that can become a spirit, which, when harnessed, is worth more than any million-pound signing. We had it at Dundee, where everyone in our small squad knew they could make a contribution, but here, with a bigger squad, we now had no choice but to rely on more of those players who had become outcasts.

Players, like fans, are very fickle and the absolute key to all of your ideas and to maintaining that spirit is results. When things aren't going well on the pitch, that type of selfish, arrogant player will turn on you like a starving wolf, desperately seeking their opportunity to drag you down, and get rid of what they see

239

as the problem. Footballers aren't always the best at looking in the mirror and, now that results had started to turn against us a little, this group was trying to do to us what they had done to others before.

There are tell-tale signs – training standards drop, players start turning up late, coaching methods get questioned and tactics are rubbished. On the pitch the discipline is the first thing to dip, with players giving away needless, petty free kicks, kicking the ball away and berating referees. The squad arguing among themselves becomes commonplace, arms flail and others are blamed for their own failings. This is all compounded by a general lack of respect for anything to do with the club.

This was all starting to creep in and, in the space of six weeks, we drew one and lost eight games. This poor run culminated in a home defeat to Rochdale which pulled us back down towards the bottom four. We had reached the dizzy heights of 10th just a couple of months earlier but, as always at football clubs, over-performing only serves to build unrealistic expectations. Now that the wolves were back into the team we couldn't buy a win and the pressure was on. Five clean sheets out of six and picking up 23 points from 36, beating Sunderland in the FA Cup and taking Man City to a replay were all now a distant memory, but we were still up for the fight.

Having had a taste of the big time, I wasn't going to give it up lightly to go back to my 14-hour shifts on the site. However, in the background, the 'old guard' were working their ticket. Murmurings of the coaching being poor, training being average and no one liking the manager were all being fed back through various staff channels from disruptive players who couldn't see that their lack of ability and bad attitude made them culpable. The outcome was inevitable. The atmosphere became poisonous, the loan window and any chance we had of improving the squad was shut. This was a board who were famous for pulling the trigger a few short months before the season ended in order to get that so-called 'reaction' from a new manager. Why should we expect things to be different this time?

Our usual Saturday evening routine was to leave at 6pm for the five-hour journey to Glasgow so we could spend Sunday with the family before driving back at 5.30am on Monday. We could tell something was amiss right after that Rochdale game when we couldn't find anyone to say goodbye to. There were no directors about, the chief executive wasn't around for his usual chat and the chairman was nowhere to be seen. We made the journey back up the road, but I could sense things weren't normal and, by the time we reached my house for the drop off, Alex had received a phone call from the gaffer to say that he'd been called to a meeting on Sunday. Paul being Paul, with his strength of character and no-nonsense approach, told them that he wouldn't be turning up and if they had anything to tell him, they could tell him over the phone. And that was it. He was sacked, no mutual consent, no ceremonial parting of the ways. He was plainly and simply sacked.

Alex and I had actually been given that coming Monday off so we could attend the funeral of a friend's mother, but we had no choice except to travel straight back down to Nottingham the very next day

241

as someone had to take training in Paul's absence. It was difficult having to tell one of our best friends that we wouldn't make the funeral, but we were left with no option. We eventually managed to get hold of the chief executive when we stopped at the Scotch Corner services and he confirmed that we should turn up on Monday to take training alongside the new caretaker manager. We were surplus to requirements, but would be made to suffer for another week. That the caretaker was the current chief scout, who just so happened to be the chief executive's best pal, was contemptible, but with a severance payment depending on us fulfilling our legal obligations, we were in no position to rebel.

We continued to work throughout the week, advising the caretaker on training methods and potential problems as we prepared for an away game at Dagenham that Saturday, but the depths the players were stooping to was disgraceful. There was a smugness about them, almost a pride that they had managed to get their way again. It was difficult to look some of them in the eye as I walked along the corridor to the dressing room, never mind prepare them for a match, but there was no other option. My personal pride meant I had to give the new guy my respect and do my best for him. Alex and I agreed that it wasn't his fault he'd been elevated to a position out of his depth and we would do our best to try to galvanise what was left of the squad for the game.

Someone should have told the players.

They were 3-0 down and reduced to 10 men by half-time and the new guy wanted to go all-out attack to get back in the game. We advised him it would be suicide and keeping things tight and hitting on the

242

break was the best way to approach the second half. A 3-1 full-time result restored some respectability but, by Monday morning, a new manager was in the process of being appointed and we were on our way.

When it came to coming to agreement on a compensation package, the club were incredibly professional. The League Managers Association in England has enough power to dictate that no new gaffer can be employed until the previous incumbent's severance has been agreed. If the same rules were applied in Scotland, clubs would be prevented from abusing contracts and starving managers and coaches into accepting reduced compensation, like Dundee tried with me.

It took us 15 minutes to come to an agreement with the Notts County managing director and I walked away with the six-month severance package that was to become my next rainy day account. It was to County's enormous credit that they did things so quickly and so amicably. We told the MD that the club's philosophy of hiring and firing wasn't sustainable, that the players would continue to cause problems so long as they were overpaid for this level, and that such instability would eventually cost the club a lot of money and fans in the long term. He agreed, but reminded us that he was a long-time friend and business associate of the chairman and that he didn't make the decisions, only worked out the figures.

When managers are sacked they'll always trot out the old cliches about how they 'wish the club every success in the future' or how they 'will be following their results' or that they 'had a great relationship with the club'. More often than not in reality you

243

leave a club with resentment and hope that the next manager bombs because anything other than that makes you look a failure. I certainly wasn't desperately wishing for a Notts County success story after we left Meadow Lane.

Since Paul Ince was sacked in 2011, Notts County have gone through another four full-time managers and three caretaker appointments, narrowly avoiding relegation each year before finally succumbing to the drop at the end of the 2014/15 season. Ten of the players we inherited and who we identified very early in our tenure as not being good enough were no longer playing League football the following season. There's a great old saying in Glasgow that 'you can only piss with the cock you've got'. Some football clubs need to understand this and remember that even those with the biggest cocks need to look in the mirror sometimes.

When you're playing football the only pressure on you is that you have to perform for 90 minutes, once or twice a week. You have a natural talent, a skill and an ability that has managed to take you this far and you alone are the one who will dictate whether or not you can pull it off in a match. That's the key difference between playing and managing/coaching. When you're playing, you only have to trust yourself. Do your best and play well, then everything will be okay. But when you're on the other side of that white line you can perform to the best of your ability all week and set everything up perfectly, only for someone else to let you down. You have to trust your judgement, your team selection, your staff and your players and that's where the pressure comes in. No matter what level you're working at, you will never be able to trust EVERYONE to do their job, particularly at a club where there's more back-stabbing going on than at a blind samurai convention.

And, to top it all off, you MUST succeed. That success could be challenging for a title, securing a top-six place or staving off relegation but, regardless of what the target is, the pressure becomes intense. Three dodgy results and you're staring the ignominy of the dole queue in the face again. One defeat can mean that horrible, debilitating feeling of isolation, standing at the side of the pitch with worries of being sacked overcoming the fear of whether or not your opponents are going to score at the next corner.

The only way I can describe it is the feeling of being claustrophobic and stuck in a lift full of people. The only air left to breathe is in the space above you and, with every floor, and each addition, the air is diminishing. Except the floors are matches and the lift is a stadium and, whether there are 250 people or 25,000 in the ground, every one of them is sucking the oxygen from around you. With every goal that flies past your hapless defence you get closer to suffocating. They're looking at you, they're all looking at you and begging you to turn it around. You vow to work harder and fight to save your position but by now the elevator is dropping like a stone and, no matter how many buttons you press, it's not stopping.

I'm not even claustrophobic.

And the feeling isn't even confined to the ground. You take it home with you, constantly pre-occupied and short tempered. The kids wonder what they've done wrong when an innocent request for some 'Dad and Hannah' time is met with a snarl. All you can think about is staying in a job. What do we do this week? Will we change training? Who's fit? What waste of space is injured again? HOW LONG WILL WE GET???

Night time is the worst. Wide awake at 3am, thinking about team formations and results. Even when you're winning you're only ever one or two results away from the fans mounting your back again, so the pressure to keep doing well is equally intense.

Constantly apologising at night for keeping Samantha awake, I'd go downstairs and perversely put on Sky Sports News to keep my mind off the football. Allan Preston told me that, when he was manager of Livingston, he'd keep a pen and paper at the side of his bed so that when he woke up (which was inevitable) he could keep a note of what he'd been thinking about so he wouldn't forget it in the morning.

I've heard fans say 'that's not REAL pressure, real pressure is when you can't put food on the table' on numerous occasions and 'you can't be feeling pressure when you're being paid so much' just as many times. Unless you've managed to stumble upon this chapter without reading the rest of the book, you'll know that I was never exactly rolling in it. I know what only ever being two or three games from signing-on again means to most people in the game.

I'm also aware that just because someone was at the opposite end of the earnings scale to me it doesn't mean they're immune from that very real, very suffo-

246

cating pressure. Before I started coaching, I bumped into my old teammate Andy Watson, then assistant manager at Rangers. Over a beer he talked about the stresses of the role. They had just won the treble but were going through a tough period, the following season when Celtic were dominating and, in Andy's words, he and his gaffer Alex McLeish were under pressure. In my naivety I said things couldn't be that bad as he was earning a few quid for his troubles.

'Faz,' he said. 'You have no idea.' He was right, I didn't. I'd fallen into the fan trap of thinking that, just because someone was being paid well, the pressure was off. Having since experienced what he was trying to get across, I can only imagine what kind of stresses he and his family were going through at a club that size and with the demands placed on it. The footballing rewards are rarely commensurate for the pressure that management and coaching bring. We all feel it, from top to bottom, and the only thing that diminishes it is success. Briefly.

I'd now been part of five sacked management teams, but at least I was back home and the road back to Glasgow had brought with it an epiphany. Samantha had been a rock once again, making sure things had run smoothly at home, looking after the kids whilst still managing to do her course at college. It was something she'd always wanted to do and, for once, rather than me being the one who got to follow the dream, this was her turn. I should have been able to support her better, but the minute the Notts County job had come up I selfishly left her holding the baby, literally, once again. The kids were now five and eight and deserved more stability in their lives. Samantha deserved more stability, so I took a conscious decision to do something about the way we lived. Two-and-a-half years of full-time employment and then nine months out of work, six months employment and then more time out fighting for compensation, living on the breadline and existing hand to mouth. It couldn't continue.

I called Brian at the end of April to see if he still had a place for an old, washed-up, unemployed coach in his Synthetic Grass Solutions empire and, fortunately, he was able to give me a start again. The first job we had was to replace the old, red blaes track at Cappielow with a nice, new synthetic rubber surface. This stuff came in 25kg bags and was mixed with an epoxy solution in a cement mixer, which when laid, hardened and became the athletics track surfaces you see today. You couldn't get this stuff on your body as it stuck and turned black. We had to wear chemical suits and masks that looked like they'd been lifted from the set of CSI Miami.

For two weeks we re-laid the target greens at a driving range in Bothwell from 6-11am before heading to Cappielow, where we'd don the forensic suits and batter on until 7pm. They were long, gruelling, hot demanding days and the final nail in the coffin came on Morton's first day back for pre-season training. Their manager Allan Moore and his assistant Mark McNally, both good friends of mine, came back to the stadium to have a look at how things were progressing with their new track. The first thing that confronted them was a spaceman; an eerie figure in a full-body white chemical suit and breathing mask, pouring blue rubber crumb into a mixer. They never

248

even recognised me. I took down the hood and lifted the mask and they never had to say anything, the look on their faces said it all. They were shocked, and although they would never say so, they had that sympathetic, almost pitiful, look that told me they were feeling sorry for me and asking themselves how I had ended up like this.

They knew I was working for Brian, but I don't think they had quite realised what it sometimes entailed. I was a fighter and I was providing for my family but as I stood there in my steel toecaps and protective gloves and listened to their pre-season preparations and aspirations for the year ahead, I'd never felt so lonely. I was embarrassed and that wasn't me. Never in my football career, nor in my life, did I worry about what other people thought. 'Fuck them' had always been one of my mottos because I was determined and knew what I had to do to make it. But now life had turned full circle and I felt weak and self-conscious.

I imagined Allan and Mark whispering about how it was a shame that I had to work for a living as they walked away. The reality was that I did, but that particular line of work wasn't for me anymore. I made a decision that night to change. I could handle the physical, tough manual labour and there was a satisfaction about being able to slog for 12 hours in the sun and go home at night, hungry, but pleased that you had got the job done. I didn't think I was too good for the job either. Brian had done a fantastic job building his company and his employees were good at what they did and knocked their pan in for their families. The truth was I couldn't take the humiliation of working at football grounds all the time anymore. It meant explaining to all my old pals that I was no longer in football. I'll be eternally grateful to Brian for giving me work when I was in desperate need of it, but I knew I needed a new career.

The problem is that there's not many things a footballer is qualified to do. I couldn't afford to take time out and learn a new trade or go to college. I had to earn money from day one and it had to be steady, guaranteed income. Over the years I'd somehow managed to maintain the ruse that I still had a few quid. Few of my mates would ever have realised how much of a struggle it had been at times. I would even lend some of them money on the odd occasion just because I couldn't bear to tell them I didn't have it to spare. It's strange how I'd never been a materialistic person and yet fought to keep up the pretence that I wasn't skint. After all, I was a footballer and everyone thought we were loaded. I couldn't let them down with something as boring as the truth.

It was difficult for me but I had to accept that, after 26 years, I was drifting out of the game. Yet, despite everything, I still wasn't willing to give up on football altogether. A lot of my pals worked as taxi drivers and, as you didn't need any formal qualifications for the job, it seemed a logical step. The biggest lure of all was that it would allow me the flexibility to take a part-time coaching role should one materialise. I was realistic to know that getting back into football full-time was unlikely. My profile wasn't particularly high and, having had a couple of what would be seen as failures to my name, I would have to go it alone from the bottom to prove myself worthy of a position all over again.

By now Alex had been working alongside Ricky Sbragia with some of the Scotland youth squads and was doing some scouting work for for MK Dons again. There had been some talk of him being in the running at both Kilmarnock and St Mirren, but I knew he'd a hankering to stay in England and unless he got a full-time management position up here, I'd be better off concentrating on trying to get my taxi driver's licence. That way, if I did somehow land a full-time gig then I could be back behind the wheel the day after the inevitable sacking without worrying about having to go to court or fighting for my next pay cheque.

After dinner I would lock myself away upstairs for three or four hours every night and work away. It wasn't London, far from it, but the scale of what is required is enormous. You have to learn where EVERYTHING is – not just the streets and the famous landmarks – you need to learn the auction houses, the banks, industrial estates, hospitals, hotels, pubs, health centres and places of interest. There are 90 districts in Glasgow and you need to know them all, more than 360 main roads and you need to know where they are and what streets link them at their beginning and end. It was a topographical nightmare and a mind-numbing task.

On average only 30 per cent of those who start studying for the test, actually sit it. Of those, only 30 per cent reach the 80 per cent pass mark. When I received my results I did that thing we all do when

251

checking to see if the coupon is up or not, covering your eye so only half the page is visible before finding the team your hopes are pinned on and slowly moving across the page trying to squeeze a '0' into somehow becoming a '3'. Anyway, on this occasion, I opened the envelope with more trepidation than I ever felt as a schoolkid. The ritual began, slowly removing the contents from the envelope with sweaty palms and then opening the letter as my heart raced.

This could determine my family's future but, just as importantly, my own sanity. I had my heart set on this now and couldn't go back to the constant calluses on my hands and a back that was, by now, stiffer than that sock hidden under a teenager's bed. I edged it out a little further, it looked like an '8' but it could still be a '6'. I must be sick in the head, putting myself through this and prolonging the pain. 'Fuck it!' I opened it all the way and quickly scanned the contents – '86 per cent'. That was the most important thing I could see. I screamed in the living room, a huge 'yaaaaaaassssssss!!!' A startled Samantha ran through wondering what on earth was going on as I hadn't told her the results had arrived. I was overjoyed. I'd scored the odd goal and won important games in my career, but the feeling of both joy and relief I currently had just about matched anything I had ever felt playing.

For the next year or so, I was strangely contented. I was out of football and, whilst I was working long, unsociable hours, at least I was away from the pressures that went with being in the game and was going home to Samantha and the children every night. I'd occasionally be recognised by football supporters who got in the cab and have a bit of banter. Celtic, Rangers, Thistle, Hibs and Hearts fans alike. Sure there was the odd Rangers fan who would give me a bit of abuse because of my background and the Jambos were great fun when they came through to Hampden for a big game, but it was almost always good-natured and light-hearted. As I always told them, if you can take it from 50,000 at Ibrox then it shouldn't be a problem to take it from one or two in the street.

For some reason, being a taxi driver was deemed more acceptable to football people and I didn't get the same pitying looks as I did when laying artificial grass. And the only time I had to don a forensic suit was to clean up after someone had brought the contents of their Saturday night up on the cab floor. Things were looking up.

Samantha reckoned I was a nicer person now I'd stopped worrying about a bad result or who would replace an injured player, or wondering where the next win bonus was coming from. Financially I was keeping things ticking over. We certainly weren't well off, but at least if things needed paid I could work an extra shift and not need to worry too much about it.

My football fix was being provided by Lewis and I going to Celtic Park together on a Saturday (or as often as not Sunday due to Sky's ridiculous scheduling), just as my Dad and I had all those years ago. I loved being a supporter again. We all have our match day rituals, getting up early and getting changed into your lucky shirt and the rest of your match clothes. Meeting at the same time and then making your way

253

to the same lamp post before heading to the same pub. Ordering the same drink and then sitting down and slagging the same mate, who every week avoids getting his round in. Walking the same, well-worn route to the ground. Then there's the same mate who can't make it to the stadium without stopping for a pee and has to nip down the same lane. And you walk in the same turnstile and take the same seat, only stopping briefly to shake the hand of everyone who sits around you, the only exception being the guy who you fell out with three seasons previously because he does nothing but berate the team and you couldn't take it anymore. My football world had turned full circle, I was a punter again and here I was introducing my son to the game. My family life was happy, settled and stable.

The bags under my eyes were returning to being just a shadow rather than the refuse sacks they had become. I was happy and I was being the partner and father my family deserved so, when the call came, of course I was willing to risk this new-found domestic bliss and put my family through the wringer one more time.

I'd been tipped off by an agent that Willie McStay might be giving me a call. It's something that goes on a lot behind the scenes in football when players get the polite 'just wanted to know if you would be interested in going to ... at the end of the season' query. It's an illegal approach, of course, but it's common practice all the same. My circumstances were different. It was unlikely that any of the drivers on the rank would object to me having been tapped up to go and ply my trade elsewhere. In fact, most of them would have been delighted to see one less taxi driver on the road touting for business.

A non-league club in Carlisle had been taken over by Frank Lynch, a US-based, Glasgow-born multi-millionaire, after a chance meeting when the team/supporters' bus broke down on the motorway. The upshot of it all was that Frank, who HAD wealth off-the-radar, was prepared to bankroll this team, Gilford Park, all the way from the ninth tier of English football, through the pyramid system into the League proper. It was an absolute fairytale, of course, and one not dissimilar to what had happened a few miles north at Gretna, but the money was being paid up front for decent signings from the Scottish and English leagues.

It would take five straight promotions to catapult a Northern League side into League Two and this particular club currently played in front of around 100 people, so the owner's idea was to harvest support from the Irish, Welsh and Scottish communities in the Carlisle area. To do this the club would be renamed Celtic Nation FC – that's Celtic pronounced with a 'K'. To further their profile, the team would play in green and white hoops and, as a result, it was hoped that Celtic, pronounced with an 'S', supporters would also be enticed to come along to watch 'The Nation'. There were rumours circulating at the time the club was to be a vehicle for Celtic to gain entry into the English League by way of taking over the club's license once they had gained their promotions. I have to say that takeover scenario was never mentioned by anyone within the club and, as far as I'm aware, it was nothing more than speculation, but it certainly never did the club any harm in the short term.

Appointing Willie as manager was a clever move by the owners because in one fell swoop they would get an experienced and respected coach who would appeal to the Celtic, with an 'S', support they were clamouring for. I'd only met Willie in passing over the years at various matches, but he'd been given my name, along with a list of others, as someone who might fit the bill for the assistant manager's role. I had the experience and the Celtic-supporting background so when I met Willie, I made sure I sold myself on that basis. There was a couple of hundred quid a week on offer and a promotion bonus which would adequately cover the time I would miss working. We hit it off and Willie seemed to like the fact I was very honest with him. I told him I would be the most loyal, hard-working assistant he could want. I'd stand shoulder to shoulder with him and do as much or as little as he required of me.

I'd immerse myself in the position as much as I could but, in a sign that my new-found status as a family man wasn't a fraud, I wouldn't commit to any more than two nights and a Saturday. My (real) work was my priority now and, for once, the coaching job would be a side project. It must have worked because within a few days he called and offered me the job. Now I just had Samantha to contend with.

I told Willie I would go away and do my sums (which meant somehow manoeuvring myself into a position where Samantha couldn't convince me not to take the job). My sales pitch was the same as always; Willie had a terrific name in the game and, if we did well, there could be the opportunity to get a bigger, better job. Samantha had heard all my bullshit before. This was the ninth tier of English football for fuck sake, it was hardly going to lead to the Celtic (yes, with an 'S') job. She looked at me and gave me a kiss and said nothing. She knew I would make sure the financial side of things was okay and, from the way I had tip-toed my way around the subject over the previous week, she also knew that I wanted to work with Willie. Saying nothing was her way of saying 'go for it'. So we did.

Journeymen coaches, like journeymen players, manage to accumulate a quite remarkable amount of clubs during their career. Every new name to add to their Wikipedia page brings with it new challenges, but the weather-beaten trainer will think he's seen it all before. One of the first things Willie said to me on arrival at Celtic Nation was that Steve Skinner, our 32-year-old chairman, who had recently relinquished full ownership of the club to the American owner, was playing in centre midfield. I have to confess that this was a new one on me.

I told Willie, and thankfully he agreed, that this would be his biggest problem. There would come a time when he needed to be disciplined or dropped and this would make those sort of decisions very difficult, particularly if he resented the fact we had come in and taken charge of his club.

We immediately changed the way the team played. The previous manager had believed you couldn't play football at that level, but we felt that, with players of Scottish league quality, we could beat teams with passing and quick, powerful football. We won 10 games in a row but, within the league, there was resentment at our spending prowess. Not only were we disrespecting the honourable name of the league but we were also supposedly a pair of big-headed Jocks. I couldn't have given a shit, I wanted to wipe the lot of them out and use the resentment to build a siege mentality but Willie was being clever, using his experience to attend meetings and tell them we were enhancing the profile of the Northern League.

Incredibly though, most of the resentment was coming from within the club. This was their club and they were no longer in control of it and, even though we were winning and surging up the League, the chairman and the committee made it clear they were not happy. Training kit wouldn't be ready, buses would be late, equipment would be missing, balls wouldn't be blown up and some of the local lads, who could no longer get a game, became the chairman's allies. He wanted us out and they wanted their club back. We were left with no option but to drop him.

From a football point of view he wasn't doing it anyway. He was defensively weak and if we did lose goals he was invariably at fault, but from a political point of view we had to show to the rest of the players that we weren't afraid to make big decisions. The run continued and then the chairman came to see us to tell us he was quitting as a player. It suited us just fine but I don't think we realised the damage he would eventually cause us.

Crowds were flocking in to see the Celtic Nation

258

phenomenon – 300, 400, 500, 600. There were buses from Liverpool, Larkhall, Clydebank and Hamilton coming to see us when Celtic weren't playing. Frank came over from America to watch us and brought his son and financial adviser. Even though we managed to attract 1000 people to the game, it was clear afterwards that the owner had been spooked. He wouldn't meet us and had made his way back to the hotel. Maybe it was the big crowd, maybe it was the Celtic songs being belted out or maybe it was the fact that I spotted the chairman sitting snugly with the owner's son as I took the players for their warm up. As things developed over the coming days it became clear that it was the latter.

Willie was told by Frank that he'd been told that the players didn't like him or his methods. They had a funny way of showing it as we had only lost two games in about our first 20, but it was becoming clearer that things were not as straightforward as they seemed with the takeover. The chairman clearly still had some sort of hold on the club and, even though Frank was bankrolling it, he wasn't in full control.

From my point of view, the most worrying aspect was that Frank's son was now aware of the level of spending. This was a five-year project and would take millions of pounds to complete but the message we were getting from across the water was that we were to continue as planned and go for promotion. The committee were now becoming more and more difficult, but the team just had to keep winning and we did. We pushed Spennymoor right to the line but, unfortunately, as we kept racking up the points, so did they. The Nation had an indifferent start to the

259

season before Willie was appointed and there weren't enough good teams to take points off Spennymoor, who won the title with a week to spare.

The vagaries of the Northern League were such that the champions didn't have to take promotion. It was a huge step up for a team of Spennymoor's stature to gamble on moving from a regional league to a national one and they hadn't done so on the two previous occasions they'd won the league. For some reason, they decided to stretch themselves this time but, had they not, we would have been given the opportunity as the second-placed team. There's no doubt we would have been financially better equipped and it may well have meant better contracts for myself and Willie, but there was a feeling that Spennymoor's owners were more intent on getting it up the big boys with their flash wages than they were about progressing and stretching themselves.

We had played 36 games and lost only three (including cup ties) and won the Regional Cup, the first trophy in the club's history, but I couldn't stand the narrow-minded politics of it all. I couldn't understand why the committee had sided with their chairman and why they couldn't see the bigger picture. Had they worked with us, there could've been a good job in it for them, a bit of prestige and an identity for the club they built, but they couldn't get the fact that Willie and I were only there to build a football team and not to take over.

After seven months, I'd had enough. I'd sacrificed a lot of my family time and more importantly, my sanity for this small, non-league entity that thought it was a football club. As the delusions of grandeur and in-fighting reached ludicrous proportions – amidst rumours, unsurprisingly, of Frank pulling his financial support – I couldn't stand the back-stabbing and lies anymore. I told Willie that I couldn't work with the chairman if he was going to still be at the club and told him I would be resigning. I'd barely spoken to Skinner since March when he threatened me with disciplinary action for telling him that I'd been in the game for 27 years and wouldn't take advice from a 32-year-old more intent on undermining the manager than moving the club forward. Willie called a few hours later to say he'd contacted the owners to pull rank and made sure the confrontation was off. With the promotion now a distant memory, thoughts turned to the following season and Willie tried to reassure me that Frank would continue his backing and that the chairman would no longer be a threat.

Frank was an honourable man and he'd given a promise to those people he met on that first day to prop up the club and make sure they were never to suffer on the back of his spending, so he felt duty bound to have another crack at it. It was madness and financial suicide to try to sustain it at that level but Willie came back from a meeting with Frank in North Carolina and set about making contact with players for the following season.

Deals were set up and pre-season friendlies organised, although my own contract was far from guaranteed as I was waiting on assurances that the former owner/player/chairman was no longer going to be involved in any capacity before I agreed to stay. And then, suddenly and inexplicably, one week later, the plug was pulled. They had their club back. I can

261

only speculate that there was some kind of deal in place behind the scenes that meant Frank never really had full control of the club. Either that or his son managed to convince him that bankrolling a virtual amateur club for the next five years was neither a sensible thing to do, nor a financially viable one.

Frank, to his eternal credit, put a package in place to ensure the club could run for the full 14/15 season. He was a bigger man than I was. After the disgraceful and disrespectful way he'd been treated, if I'd been him I'd have left them to their own devices. After cutting back severely, Celtic Nation became cannon fodder for the league and stumbled on to defeat after defeat before suffering relegation and the ultimate ignominy of folding altogether. Quite frankly, there were many people involved in the club who deserve zero sympathy for their plight.

It wasn't long before the McStay name was back in the game again, with Willie being appointed Head of Academy Recruitment at Celtic. I was pleased for him as he had showed me unstinting loyalty during that turbulent period when money, as it always does in football, had clouded normally rational people's judgements. I'd seen very early on that there was too much going on behind the scenes in order to allow things to progress so, while I gave my absolute all to Willie and the team, I hadn't quite gone 'all in'.

I was happy enough to go back to my day job without the distraction of two trips a week to Carlisle for training and one to the North East for an away game. For once, I wasn't really bothered that I was back out of the game again. Maybe I was growing up at last.

Taxi for Farrell
2015-

Retired?

Friday, 1st May 2015. There are 45,000 people at Celtic Park, but it feels empty to me. Celtic are beating Dundee 5-0 and are now just one game away from wrapping up the league yet I can't summon up any excitement. I'm not thinking about any of the 22 men on the park or anyone else in the crowd, but rather someone who isn't here. Someone who should be here, but who'll never be here again.

My Dad died last week. He didn't 'pass away', he didn't 'go to a better place', he died. After 11 days in hospital with what turned out to be a rare strain of pneumonia, he left me empty and disconsolate. I've lost the biggest influence on my career and my biggest supporter, the man I looked up to above all others, who taught me right from wrong and made sacrifices for his family.

We talk a lot about heroes and legends in football and about defeats and setbacks in terms akin to a death in the family – I've done it in this book – but when you lose your real hero you realise just how much shit we talk about the game at times. Football and family were my Dad's life but, no matter how much

265

he loved Celtic and no matter how many weekends were planned around getting to and from wherever they were playing, there was never any doubt about the order of his priorities.

The man inspired everything I did and instilled in me the socialist, working-class, family values I try to live by to this day. Football tested those principles to the limit, but the grounding that James Patrick Farrell gave me kept me from being corrupted by the back-stabbing, cheating and ruthlessness that went on, even if I wasn't immune to the selfishness that's common to almost everyone in the game. Instead of sympathising with managers who'd given me a chance when they faced the sack, I would be half-excited about what it might mean for me. What was many times worse was putting my family's security at risk by continuing to chase my dream and being less than honest about money with my wonderful, loving and supportive partner.

Most people will, I think, understand my desire to be a professional footballer and to stay in the game for as long as possible, even at the obvious cost to my own health. It was all I'd ever wanted to do and no one will ever be able to take those 18 years away from me. Whatever I got out of the game I worked my arse off for, but it was all worth it to me. What I think they'll find more difficult to fathom was my determination, or perhaps desperation, to stay in coaching in spite of all the administrations, liquidations and sackings and all the hardships and difficulties that went with it. For Samantha, who was beside me at every stage, even considering a return to the cut-throat, insecure and stressful world of coaching was, at best, masochistic and, at worst, suicidal. She was right, of course, there was no reasonable explanation as to why anyone would want to put themselves or their family, through that again.

Every opportunity in coaching that I pitched as the golden ticket, I believed I was doing it for her and the kids. I believed those part-time numbers were for them, two nights and a Saturday out of the home in the hope that it would lead to the next step on the ladder. I believed missing out on Lewis and Hannah growing up so I could spend six days a week battling a dressing room in Nottingham was the right thing to do for them, but all I was doing was putting pressure on myself and my family. What I've now come to realise is that I was doing it for myself, for my own selfish desire to stay in football. Sam knew this all along of course, but she never said it and never stopped me from pursuing my dream/fantasy.

And now? I've not worked in football for well over a year at the time of writing. That's the longest I've been out the game since I joined Oxford as a trainee nearly 30 years ago and that's okay because football isn't the be all and end all for me now. There's been the odd job mentioned that didn't come off, but it's not the end of the world. It's no longer my priority. If nothing ever came up in football again I can honestly say it wouldn't bother me.

Writing my blog has led to this book, and one or two wee things in the media that I enjoy. I'm back going to see Celtic every second week and Lewis and I sit about 15 yards from the spot on the terraces where my Dad used to take me when I was his age. Football is tribal, and long may that be the case. It's in our blood and we pass this obsession from one generation to another. The death of my Dad put football into perspective like never before, but that doesn't mean I'll ever agree that it's just a game. If it was, then fans wouldn't go back year after year knowing that disappointment was likely, if not inevitable. If football was just a game then you wouldn't have lasted nearly 300 pages of me going on about how I never made it to the top.

It would take a very, very good offer to disrupt the settled family life I've got now. But the fact football isn't just a game but a drug means I still can't bring myself to rule out the prospect of the phone ringing, me making my pitch to Samantha, and her thinking 'oh no' all over again. An addict is always an addict, even if they're no longer using.

I wake up in the morning and I'm not sure whether my left foot or my left knee will be the more painful that day. The right side of my body actually isn't too bad, but the left is wrecked, the legacy of those injuries and those injections I lied to medical staff to get. I should also wear orthotic inserts to help me walk a bit more steadily at times. To me, this was just the price I had to pay to be able to play football for a living.

The bizarre thing is that, even when you're actually playing, football is very often not fun. You're so involved in it, in every aspect of your performance, your standing at the club and your fitness that you can't even tell if you're enjoying yourself anymore. It's only when you win at the end of it that it becomes fun but the playing, managing, coaching, pressure and expectations overtake that for much of the time.

The good part is winning, but the day-to-day activity isn't necessarily great to take part in and it's all just the means to the ultimate end. It can, of course, be enormously enjoyable but it's also far more intense than those outside the inner circle realise.

For me, and thousands like me, it means playing at a level when you're never going to make your fortune or lap up glory. It means fighting every day just to stay where you are because you know there are countless other journeymen waiting for you to fail and to take your place. It means endless politics and back-stabbing and sleepless nights. It means putting your body on the line for clubs who'll toss you onto the scrapheap the second they think they can get away with it.

It's the best job in the world.

A massive amount of thanks are due to the following people:

To my Mum and Dad for instilling in me the discipline and morals I tried to carry through my life and career.

To Angela and John who made it very easy to be a big brother, and to James, we still miss you.

To Samantha for putting up with me and all my shit over the years, for all your incredible support and for never once wavering as I chased my dream.

To Lewis and Hannah for making me proud and for being such amazing, clever, conscientious children.

To Harris. It wasn't always easy, but we got there and I'm incredibly proud of how you've stood on your own two feet and hope I've helped with that along the way.

To Frank and Isabel Forrester for all the parties and for allowing me to sing at them.

To Jim Burke for nudging me in the right direction, and Sierra Fong and Paul McGeary for all their help.

To Bill Leckie, Gordon Waddell, Michael Gannon, Neil Cameron, Michael Grant, and, especially, Kenny MacDonald for their professional opinion and encouragement that I could do this.

To Irvine Welsh for telling me that I was actually quite good and for making tennis commentary infinitely less boring

To Alex Rae and Phil McQuillan for being there for me through the last 30 years, and extra thanks to Alex for all the opportunities you gave me.

To Grant Hill and Frank Marra at Teckle for being unswerving in their belief in me through this whole writing process and supporting me during one of the most difficult months of my life. I will never forget that.

To all the other people who helped make this book possible – Ryan Norrie, Chris Collins, Linda Isles, Ranald Henderson, Ryan Law, Bob McDevitt, David Young, Robert Reid, George Peters, Richard Watt, Alan Cheghall and Mike Garty

And finally, to wee Amy Jane, for being the newest, brightest star in my sky.

ALSO AVAILABLE FROM TECKLE BOOKS

The Tartan Special One
Barry Phillips

"Boundlessly imaginative, gleefully silly, occasionally nightmarish and always inventively filthy, The Tartan Special One is by some distance the funniest book I've read in years." **Christopher Brookmyre**

"A hoot from start to finish. Rip roaring comedy with a phantom serious edge and beautiful ending."
Irvine Welsh

Lloyd George dreams of playing for his beloved Manchester United and lapping up the adulation of millions of fans across the globe. So when Dundee FC chairman Bob McCracken, a man of vision, ambition and moderately priced suits, offers Lloyd the chance to play his part in restoring the once-proud club to its rightful place in Scottish football, the shy 17-year-old sees it as a stepping stone to bigger things.

Instead he finds himself drawn into a battle for football's very soul waged by Jocky, the team's moustachioed, monomymous and megaphone-wielding manager, and seeking solace between the thighs of Dundee's first female binman.

A hilarious satire on the "Coldplaification" of the beautiful game, The Tartan Special One asks the big important questions and a load of wee shitey ones as well. It's pure teckle, aye?